PAY ATTENTION!

A POWERFUL GUIDE TO THE WORLD

SUSAN D. MATZ

Pay Attention!

Published by Heart Studios Inc.
1522 Plum Lane
Westmont, IL 60559

ISBN: 978-0-9817974-0-3

Printed in the United States of America

10   9   8   7   6   5   4   3   2
1

Contents

*To move through the world
powerfully,
you first have to know
the world*

Preface

Life is an energy that moves us forward. Mankind is an ever-evolving being, and the process of life is one of the things that help us to evolve by challenging us to keep up. We've gone from a purely physical existence way back in those "caveman" years to the arts, then science, and now we're entering the age of deeper meaning. "What's it all about?" is where we're going next. We've learned how to move through the world (our physical selves), how to create in the world (our artistic selves), how to work in the world (our mental selves) and now we're learning how to live in harmony, or conjunction, with the world. Harmony is just another way to say balance, a state where things that can seem very opposing find a space to work in sync with one another.

In people, balance is achieved when the mind, body and passion are connected to a person's inner purpose. You see this in athletes when they have those moments where they just seem one with what they're doing. They fly into the air like they have wings, making it all look so graceful, easy and peaceful. In that moment, it's all in balance for them. Their mind, body, passion and purpose are in sync. It's a beautiful thing to witness, and even more beautiful to experience personally.

Globalization is the process of connecting the world together through things like our economics, travel and socialization (which was given a huge boost by the Internet). Finding balance here is just as important as finding personal balance. But natural globalization (humanity being interconnected without actively working on it, like using the Internet) has always been there, most people have just never seen how it affected their lives. An obvious example of natural globalization is our planet. No matter what country you live in, when you put something damaging into the atmosphere it affects the atmosphere of the entire planet, not just the immediate sky above you. When you dump toxins into the ocean, the entire ocean is affected, and since the ocean affects every piece of land mass on the planet along with weather patterns, at some point it physically impacts everyone, and not in a good way.

We are interconnected and this has always been the case, but now is the time in our evolution for mankind to really understand this concept at a deeper level. The first lessons are coming in physical form, meaning people are being challenged to look at how interconnected everything is by facing things like our deteriorating global environment (global warming) and dangerous weather pattern changes. Economy, trade and information (like Internet-sharing sites where millions of people log on daily) are also challenging people all over the planet to understand how one thing can affect everything else in the world. Once people understand that things are globally connected, they can start looking at things like the deeper meaning behind it all and how to find balance globally, not just personally.

Globalization plays a huge part in the next level of our evolution. Humanity has to find its personal balance (that's the journey each person goes through on their own to understand their place and purpose in the world), its interpersonal balance (that's different countries, societies, economies, religions, etc., learning to flow together) and its balance with the planet itself. The multiple growing crises in things like our environment, tensions between countries and increasing individual violence is showing us that as a whole, humanity is not in balance. Part of balance is depth; you have to go look at things like the "why" behind what you're doing. Yes, you want a new car, but why? Do you need it or does your ego just want it? And when you do buy a car what kind of emissions are you putting into the environment, because that car isn't just about you, its emissions are affecting every living being in the world, so what are you putting out in the world? And do you really have the money to buy that car, because if you don't and you end up going into bankruptcy then you're making other people literally pay for your financial mistake.

Everything is interconnected, and the next level in mankind's journey is to help people understand this and be more conscious, which means taking deeper personal responsibility for what you're doing in life, because much of what you do affects everyone else on some level.

This book is a general guide to paying attention to the world around you. It's not filled with tons of facts, because those would be outdated before the book even got published (so the "facts" in here are already old information!); instead, it's filled with generalized information and generalized concepts about the world in which you live in order to help you connect more.

Mankind is being challenged to grow up and take responsibility for the world it lives in, and the things it does in this world. That means you, as an individual, can take more personal responsibility for understanding your own country, how it works, what effect it has on the rest of the world, what is going on in the rest of the world and why it all matters. It's time to grow up and be present in the world that you have created, or there just might not be a world to create in down the road.

Susan D. Matz

Awareness

How many countries are there on the planet? How many different languages? How many different types of government, and how do they work? How does the government in the U.S.A. work? What makes up Congress, and how does it run? How many subcommittees are there, what are they, and what do they do? Can you explain the difference between the Republican Party and the Democratic Party? Who are the five most powerful people in the federal government and why? What's the difference between a town and a city, and why does it matter? How does the tax system work? What is NASDAQ? How does the economy work in this country? What's the national debt and how is it broken down? How about the debt of the state you live in? What's the difference between privatization of our healthcare system and a national healthcare system? How many known dictators are there in the world and what countries do they rule over? What defines a dictator? Which countries have nuclear capability? What's the United Nations, when was it founded, and what's its purpose? How many people live on the planet, and how many (*one half of the world's population!*) live in poverty? On 9/11 the U.S. discovered what it was like when terrorists attack on a large scale, something many other countries have dealt with for years, but did you know that there had been other terrorist attacks here? And when 9/11 happened, many complaints came out about the U.S., including our "foreign policies," which many people in other countries claim is the reason behind why they "hate the U.S.A.," but can you name even one U.S. foreign policy? How about those causing so much rage outside this country? You're not alone; most people can't answer any of these questions.

Americans are some of the most educated yet ignorant people on the planet. We're often educated in a skewed system that is based on getting you a job that pays well, not in understanding yourself, life or the world in which you live. This lack of understanding is literally becoming deadly. The world is interconnected, and what this country does that affects other countries in a detrimental way is coming back to haunt us, but because most Americans have no idea about the links between us and other parts of the world they don't understand the anger, resentment and hostility that some people have for Americans. There's a naïve American mentality that this is the "best" country and "everyone wants to be an American," but it's not true. Yes, America is a great country, but so are many others on the planet. America's not perfect; no place is. Like everything else in the world it has its good points and its bad. If you can't see the problems, you can't fix them. So if you just blindly say this is a great country and nothing we do is wrong, then you're simply in denial of the serious problems that exist.

Owning up to problems is the path toward changing them into something potentially spectacular. Ignoring or covering up problems not only stops evolution, it actually causes people's maturity level to decrease and evolution to halt. Ignoring problems creates the biggest problem of all: no more real advancement in life, just false cycling in denial. Evolution and change go together. If you can't face, deal with and participate in changing what isn't working, there is no forward movement in life.

Everything you do affects other people. This is not an original statement. Many people have been saying it for many years, but for most it's just a concept. People are just beginning to understand how their actions affect other people. Mankind evolves from learning about itself; *no* learning equals *no* evolution. So if you don't learn to understand how what you say and do affects so much more than just yourself, then you're going to be left behind as the rest of mankind leaps forward in evolution. And not only is there no evolution forward, bad things happen when you don't really understand what's going on, because in a state of ignorance, you just keep doing something harmful without really seeing the harm you're causing. It's like a parent using the word "stupid" a lot around their children, like saying, "Oh come on, that's just stupid," or "Don't be stupid, put that over there and set it down." It could be twenty or more years before that now adult child goes back and tells the parent that their low self-esteem and inability to hold down a job is directly related to the thousands of casual "stupid" statements that all added up to deteriorate their self-confidence. In a more short term example, someone is gabbing on their cell phone and goes through an intersection on a green light and right into a funeral procession that was going by. Yes, the light was green, but the other cars weren't moving for a reason – the funeral procession – but the person who went through the intersection wasn't paying attention to their driving because they were on the phone, and now many lives are changed forever. You are interconnected in your immediate surroundings and on a *global* level. The more you understand this, the healthier choices you make in this world, and the better effect you have on the world. First you have to see the effect you have on your more immediate surroundings, then your mind can grasp the deeper effect you have in this world.

This is not a book to tell you what to do, to fill you with "facts" about the world you live in or give you quick answers about how to go out and fix the world. I'm not a sociologist, economist, political activist or anything like that. I'm an educator who has taught, among other things, the value of understanding yourself, your life purpose and the world in which you live. The world does not change because some sweeping "one solution fits all" thing happens. Change is a process just like anything else, and it happens one person at a time. Time changes nothing, people do. And people don't change as a group, it takes one person at a time becoming more aware, getting involved and making better choices.

Information

Information is a very powerful thing, and there's a lot of it out there in the world, but most of that information never makes it into usable knowledge. People aren't fully aware of what's going on, so there's a lot of unused information floating around that could be used to help change the world in a great way, but isn't. Mankind has so much potential, but right now we're not using it.

The world changes one person at a time. There is no large reform that can make large change happen because the world is made of individual people, and they have to change for any real large change to occur. And in order for real change to occur, not just superficial and temporary behavioral changes, you have to be aware of both yourself and the world in which you live. Awareness is a broader state than just having a bunch of information or facts in your head. Awareness is a state where you <u>understand</u> what's going on, and you don't necessarily need technical information to really understand something. If you don't really understand what's going on, then all the detailed, technical information in the world doesn't mean a thing.

You can't change what you don't understand. And when you're not aware of what's going on in the world, then you can't understand your individual connection to it. Twenty years ago many people mocked the idea of recycling because they didn't see the cumulative effect of not recycling. They didn't see the gigantic landfills or tie together the connection between the toxic gases coming off those landfills to the deteriorating weather conditions and global warming. Twenty years ago most people thought that "global warming" just meant the weather was getting hotter, so who cares? They didn't understand the effect it has on weather patterns, fresh water and the potential destruction of this planet in the future because the atmosphere is being destroyed. Even today people are having a hard time getting out of the limitation of just seeing the world through the filter of their own personal lives, and only seeing their lives today, not how it affects tomorrow. People are struggling to connect their daily choices and habits with the potential harm and destruction it's connected to.

How many of the products that you've purchased in your life have been touched by violence, slavery, torture or abuse? "Many" is the answer to that. It's inevitable. We are interconnected in this world, especially in our economy, so all over the world there are people that were somehow involved in making what you own through things like forced labor, slavery and inhumane working conditions. Some of the choices you make today will deeply affect people you'll never meet, yet you still have a huge impact on their lives. This example is one of the darker realities in the world, but one of the many it's important to face.

People today have become too short-sighted. Two hundred years ago people forged the U.S. based on the idea of what they could create for future generations. Most of what they built they did through sweat, hard labor, war and literally giving up their own lives for future generations. Today people seem to be in the exact opposite place, only living for themselves and only living for today. They don't want to pay taxes to build a levy or a bridge that will take sixty years to complete for the next generation. If their tax dollars aren't going to be used for them within the next year, they don't want to hear about it. The U.S. was built on a foundation that understood a percentage of everything done today affects the future, for better or worse. Today that understanding is lost on many people. "Throw your garbage on the street, who cares, I won't be walking down that street tomorrow, so I won't have to see it," is more the norm. Historically people in the U.S. screamed and fought when the government stepped in on certain issues, like putting children in car seats or wearing seat belts. Remember that one? It was huge; people in our society were enraged that the law was telling them to wear a seat belt because they didn't see how their personal choice affected other people. At the time the general population would not get out of the limited way they had of looking at things.

If you get in a car accident without your seat belt on, your injuries are statistically much, much worse than someone who did wear a seatbelt. So you get in this bad car accident, and by the time you've gone through the emergency services, emergency room, ICU, step-down unit, regular floor and rehab, you could easily have wracked up over five hundred thousand dollars in costs. Yes, you have insurance, but have you paid out five hundred thousand dollars in premiums? No, you haven't, so it's a loss for both the insurance company, who now raises their rates for hundreds of thousands of people (because tens of thousands of people have gotten into very expensive car accidents due to not wearing a seat belt), and the hospital has to eat the override costs (a trauma center emergency room can be in debt for hundreds of thousands of dollars a month because of cases like this). But a hospital doesn't really "eat the cost," as people often say. They couldn't keep their doors open if they did, so they get reimbursed on both the state and federal level. That means millions of tax payers are now paying your extreme hospital bill because you didn't wear a seat belt. In the U.S., car accident deaths and related medical costs were rising and rising each year, much higher than any other country, so yes, the government stepped in to do what the people themselves weren't doing because they weren't seeing the overall or *global* problem. Most people were only seeing their limited, unaware angle of life so they felt victimized by being told what to do because they didn't see the problem.

A lack of full understanding creates a lot of problems, including blame and a feeling that you're somehow victimized. That somehow something is just "happening to you" that you didn't participate in. But you did, usually by something you didn't do rather than something you did. Like not voting, or voting for something that turns out to be a huge problem because you voted in ignorance, just taking in superficially what someone told you without really taking the time to understand what you were voting for. Life is a product of our choices. There's an old saying, "You made your bed, and now you have to lie in it." I don't know where that saying comes from, but, boy, is it true!

The more aware you are of how you connect into the world, how harmful your unawareness can potentially be and how *empowering* your awareness could be, the more passion and desire you can open up in your life to participate more. And more participation brings about more passion. In other words, the more you're aware of, the more passion you will have flowing through you to change what isn't working and come up with new ideas in the world. The more you just live for today, every day becomes the same passionless routine.

As an adult, part of your responsibility is to be aware of what's going on around you. You don't have to know everything about everything, but a little bit about the major things that take place on this planet is part of being a mature adult in the world. The more you understand, the more you're aware of what's really happening, and the more empowered you become. The less you understand, the more out of control, angry and blameful at things that go on in the world you become simply because you don't really get what's going on. Why are gas prices rising? Why is your company not giving out bonuses anymore? Why can't you sell your house for what you want? If you don't understand what's going on around you, you'll only feel angry and victimized by things like this instead of understanding the bigger picture and how it connects into your life.

This is seen a lot in the large amount of people that complain about even having to hear on the news reports of what's going on with things like the Palestinian/Israeli conflict. People don't see the connection to their daily lives, so they don't think the news should "waste my time." But there is a connection, with that conflict and so much more. Understanding this brings about maturity, passion to participate more in the world, and an increased awareness of yourself and your place in the world.

The following is a very brief description of some the major institutions, events and situations that are presently in play in our world. Some of this information may already have technical inaccuricies just because things change so fast. I want to emphasize that this is just a short synopses, simply to help bring generalized awareness to what's going on around you. There are plenty of books and other in-depth information sources that can go into each one of these in great depth, and there's a lot on the Internet that can keep you technically up-to-date if it's an area you find yourself really interested in. My intention is not to simply bring out information to people, it's to help bring awareness. Information is everywhere and constantly changing, but usually in a format that's often too complex or intense for many people to be interested in or have the time to go into because of their own daily lives.

Awareness brings about just that: a *general* awareness of what's going on. Through awareness people can open up their minds, perspectives and passion to go deeper if they should choose. You are part of this world, part of everything that is going on, whether you understand that now or not. The more aware you become, the more you can understand the world you live in and make some more conscious choices about what you want that impact to be.

General Information

- There are over six billion people on the planet.

- Half the world's population lives in two major areas: China has over one billion and India/Pakistan/Bangladesh together have almost two billion.

- There are a 194 countries, 192 belong to the UN.

- There are 61 colonies (or territories) that other countries have domain over (the U.S. holds 14 territories), and there are six long-term disputed territories (Gaza Strip/West Bank/Paracel Islands/Spratly Islands/Western Sahara/Antarctica).

- Flooding is usually the largest natural disaster to occur each year, and the UN provides around $22 million a year to natural disaster victims in the world.

- There are over two billion children in the world and half of them (every other child on this planet) live in poverty.

- In 2004, 10.6 million children died before the age of five due to poverty.

- Clean water is one of the largest humanitarian issues in the world (almost half of the population struggles with it), millions of people spend up to four hours a day walking to obtain clean water.

- Less than 500 people hold one half of the world's wealth.

- The wealthiest nation in the world (the U.S.) has the widest gap between rich and poor.

- In poor countries where they have been given "debt relief" in the form of loans, each person has to pay back about $13 for every $1 given to their government, whereas in wealthier countries international loans are paid back by the government.

- Almost half of the world's population lacks clean sanitation.

- One quarter of the world's countries combined have less wealth than the top three countries.

- One billion people cannot read or sign their names.

- There are over 200,000 children up for legal adoption around the world; (in the U.S., approximately 100,000 infertility procedures are performed every year).

ECONOMIC GLOBALIZATION

- *International Monetary Fund (IMF)* is an organization with over 180 countries as members. It was established to promote international monetary cooperation and exchange stability (trading power) to foster higher levels of growth and low levels of unemployment. It also provides assistance for countries in need by providing loans (like the World Bank) so that they can restore their economic growth. They differ from the World Bank in that they do not have specific requirements as to where the money goes, nor do they go into the country to help them build their economy.

- *World Bank (WB)* was founded in 1944 and is one of the largest sources of assistance for development in the world. This organization provides both money and ideas to developing countries to improve living standards and eliminate poverty. The representatives enter a country and work with both the government and the private sector to formulate strategies for assistance.

The World Bank is collectively owned by 184 different countries who share the same philosophy. They're run by a board of governors and a Washington, DC-based board of directors. They use their resources to send individual teams into developing countries to help educate them, create stability and growth. They focus on the poorest people and the poorest countries. They emphasize the need for health education, governing, social development, poverty reduction, private business, protecting the environment, reforms and the concept of long-term planning. Financial and social education are strong goals.

They provide bank loans to these countries with the agreement that the loan will be paid back in 15–20 years. At this time they receive less than 5% of their loans back.

- *WTO (World Trade Organization)* is an independent organization for what it calls "liberalized trading." It's a place where various governments go to work out their trade agreements. Some of the basic functions are negotiating trade agreements and settling trade disputes. One of the more difficult parts of their work involves dealing with conflicting interests. The first and largest step in this is defining what a conflicting interest is, which may sound basic, but they work with over 100 countries with various language, commerce and education issues, so defining trade conflicts, disputes and settlement issues is one of their largest jobs. They say that they are built on "neutral negotiation" and consider it their highest priority.

The WTO grew out of the *General Agreement on Tariffs and Trade,* or GATT. After WWII, fifteen countries got together to deal with tariff issues so that countries could trade more easily, increasing global economy and growth for everyone. This became GATT, born in 1945

11

in Geneva, Switzerland, and was basically the formal beginning of what we today call Economic Globalization. At the same time, fifty countries were already in talks to create an "international economy cooperation" program by combining The World Bank and IMF for the United Nations (and all three organizations were newly formed at the time). It was called the International Trade Organization (ITO). Years later the ITO would never fully make it into creation (it was the U.S.A. that ended it in 1950 because they didn't agree with some of the trade rules), leaving the GATT as the only international trade organization at the time.

One of the ways the GATT functioned was to have a series of what it called "rounds," and the rounds were named for the country they were held in, the first being in Geneva, so they were called the Geneva Rounds. These "rounds" initially consisted of negotiations, legislation and ratifications. The first round was with 23 countries. Each round added something as time went on, like anti-dumping laws or border disputes. And the countries involved showed a minimum of 8% growth in their economy, so every new round brought in more and more countries wanting to be involved. In 1986 the Uruguay Round started with 123 countries on board and lasted until 1994. By this time, the global economy, along with many other things in the world, changed so much that by the time they were done in 1994, the GATT organization had been retired and the WTO was formed out of the basic principles of things like neutrality and negotiation started with GATT. The basic principal of equal opportunity growth and respect for all countries remained a staple. Their first principle is called the "MFN (most favored nation): ... "countries cannot discriminate between trading partners ... you have to do the same for all."

- *NAFTA (North American Free Trade Agreement)* is a trade agreement between Mexico, the U.S. and Canada. It was established in 1994 with a lot of controversy around it. NAFTA replaced the Canada-U.S. Free Trade Agreement of 1988 over supposed concerns about jobs leaving this country and quality standards in trade. Among the many complaints about this agreement is that it's not considered a formal treaty in the U.S. Instead it's called a "congressional-executive agreement" and does not follow international laws, so when Canada, for example, had a significant problem with one of the trades, they found they could not sue anyone in the U.S. or get any kind of reparations. Normally treaties have a governing body and legal course that is above, or somewhat separate from, the countries system, but NAFTA, although recognized internationally as a "treaty," within the U.S. it's an "agreement," which gets them out of having a separate governing body. NAFTA was supposed to increase living conditions, especially in Mexico, increase jobs and wages, but many will tell you that the exact opposite happened. This trade agreement is disputed to this day.

- *European Union (EU)* In 1950, the process of an integrated Europe began when France proposed a European Federation. Six countries initially began it: France, Belgium, Germany, Italy, Luxemburg and the Netherlands. Today, 27 countries belong.

They state that they are based on the "law of democracy," and not on creating one large state. Their four main objectives are:

1) Establish European citizenship
2) Ensure freedom, security and justice
3) Promote economic and social progress
4) Assert Europe's role in the world

The EU is run by five institutions: a Parliament, a Commission, a Council of the Union, a Court of Justice and a Court of Auditors.

Among many things, they deal with peace relations, helping countries with their infrastructure, trade, mainstreaming Europe's currency, reforms, humanitarian aid, information, justice systems and education systems. To join, a country has to meet certain standards and agreements that the EU assists them with.

Violence

- *Child Soldiers* At any given time, there is an estimated 300,000 children being forced into war as soldiers. They are often stolen from home at a very young age, tortured and raped for years, sometimes drugged and then brainwashed with propaganda until they are detached, cold killers. Child soldiers are known to be broken down into very obedient subjects that will kill and torture others on command and without question. There are over twenty countries that routinely use and create (through torture camps) child soldiers.

- *Blood Diamonds* are formally known as "Conflict Diamonds," and refer to the connection between many African conflicts and the diamond mining industry. Impoverished, uneducated countries are sometimes referred to as having the "curse of natural resources," because they have what others want and often take through illegal or simply unethical ways. The official UN definition of conflict diamonds is…"*diamonds that originate from areas controlled by forces or factions opposed to legitimate and internationally recognized governments, and are used to fund military action in opposition to those governments.*" About 24 tons (120 million carats) of diamonds are mined a year, many under brutal conditions, unfare wages and even forced labor. Basically what happens is conflicts are started over the power and control of diamond mining.

There are 18 countries that produce diamonds; Africa holds 12 of the 18. Some of the more recent, brutal conflicts have been in Sierra Leone, Namibia, Liberia, Angola and the Congo. There are statistics that say up to 99% of all diamonds have "blood on them," but the diamond industry claims that less than 5% are from conflict. The diamond industry also states many statistics like, "ten million jobs are produced by the industry," and "five million children have healthcare because of diamond mining."

In conflict areas, the government or opposing governmental force (militias, which are the main problem) often forces people to work in the mines. Things like torture, killing family members and cutting off both hands/arms are done if the people refuse (so that they can't work anywhere else). The workers do not see the money; instead it goes to finance arms and wars that destroy these people's lives anyway. Sometimes the broker deals are made directly for arms, and no money is exchanged. The diamonds are a source of income-trade for a very large black market, but the "black market" is war.

Due to layers of well-hidden paper, it can be very hard to determine which diamonds are conflict diamonds and which ones are legitimate. For example, Australia has a very large diamond producing market that is not conflict-related. There are distinctions between diamonds and areas that they come from, so an experienced expert can tell you where a rough diamond came from. In early 2000, the Kimberly Process was started, which is a method of requiring certifications as to the history of a diamond so that the public can know if they are purchasing a blood diamond or not. So far this has not been an effective process. Because the industry keeps everything so mired down, there are virtually no statistics on blood diamonds, even the UN cannot give statistics on how many have died or been maimed by this practice.

POVERTY

- *G8* is an international forum that consists of eight industrialized countries: Canada, the U.S., Russia, Germany, Japan, the United Kingdom, France and Italy. Each year one of these countries takes on the "presidency," or responsibility of the group's yearly agenda, and at the end of the year they host a summit for all eight nations where they are supposed to make decisions based on what research was done for the year, update ongoing issues they are working on and set next year's goals. The concept for this group originated in 1973 after an oil crisis (based on relations with the Middle East) caused a recession in many countries. The U.S. created an informal group that included Japan, the United Kingdom and West Germany. In 1975, the French government invited this group along with Italy to a summit meeting and the group became known as the G6. The other countries joined later. The Leader of the European Union (which is a rotating position) has attended every summit since 1977. The topics of concern (all international) are healthcare, law enforcement, labor, economic and social development, energy, the environment, foreign affairs, justice and interior, terrorism and trade. There is also a set of meetings called the G8+5 (created in 2005), which includes China, Mexico, India, Brazil and South Africa. They are working on "a consensus to reach a post-2012 Climate Change Settlement." The Finance and Energy ministers of the G8 attend these meetings along with the current EU president.

- *UNICEF (United Nations International Children's Fund)* is a division of the UN that specifically works with aid, research and resolution of poverty in the world that affects children and families. They state that they are working for the advancement of humanity through the health and evolvement of children. They are a very large organization that works not only with crisis and poverty situations but they also work on empowering children and teenagers through things like education and challenging them to add their voices into the world. They have over 7,000 posts in 191 countries.

INTERNATIONAL AID

- *NGOs (Non-Governmental Organizations)* are small non-profit organizations dedicated to helping humanity. There are literally millions of NGOs, small private organizations that are not supposed to be affiliated with any particular government to neutrally serve mankind. In truth, some NGOs do have governmental ties to governments other than the country they're in. NGOs' methods and actions depend on their particular purpose. Some are more business-oriented and do things like technical support or lobbying, while others go out and feed the homeless or work face-to-face in impoverished areas. Some are advocacy groups, some have full-time employees, and others are purely volunteers. Under international law, NGOs are not legal entities, which brings about issues of protection for NGO members and the legality of what some of them are doing. Some NGOs, which ideally are neutral, have been known to get involved in things like coups. NGOs are also known for getting very organized and going after things like large corporations for various conditions and problems they have chosen to spotlight. In response, many large corporations have created some kind of "Socially Responsible" division; especially in today's culture of "going green," their job is to incorporate global awareness and participation. This has become so big and popular they now have acronyms like INGO for international assistance, BINGO for business assistance, ENGO for environmental assistance and TANGO for technical assistance, just to name a few. There are a lot of these organizations out there doing questionable things with questionable intentions, but most are pretty heartfelt and genuine in their intention to participate in this world by making a positive difference in some way.

* *United Nations (UN)* is an international organization that was established October 24, 1945 by 51 countries committed to preserving peace through international cooperation and international security. The term "united nations" was coined by President Theodore Roosevelt in 1942 when 26 countries pledged their governments together to fight in WWII. There are 194 recognized countries on the planet right now, 192 of which belong to the UN. The last two countries to join were East Timor (newly developed) and Switzerland in 2002.

The UN is not a "world government" and does not make laws. They take on the responsibility of what's called the UN Charter, which is an international treaty that sets up basic principals on international relationships. The UN has four purposes:
1) maintain international peace and security
2) develop friendly relations between countries
3) cooperate in solving international problems and promoting respect for human rights
4) be a center for harmonizing the actions of nations

In the UN, all members, large and small, rich and poor, with differing political views and social systems have a vote in all processes. All will be respected.

There are six main divisions. The <u>General Assembly</u> is considered a "parliament of nations," which meets to consider the most pressing problems. Each member gets one vote. In 2002, they went through 180 topics including AIDS in Africa. The <u>Security Council</u> has responsibility for maintaining international world peace. The <u>Economic and Social Council</u> coordinates social works including interfacing with all of the NGOs to maintain a link between civil organizations and the UN. The <u>Trusteeship Council</u> was established to have international supervision over the countries coming into the UN. The <u>Secretariat</u> carries out the administrative work.

The sixth division is the <u>UN System</u>, which works with fourteen organizations like the World Bank, World Health Organization (WHO) and International Labor Organization forming cooperation and unified goals. Many of the organizations it works with are older than the UN itself. This division also works with UN-based organizations and funds like the UN High Commissioner for Refugees (UNHCR), UN Development Program (UNDP) and the UN Children's Fund (UNICEF). The UN System provides communication, technical, practical, social and economic support.

The UN developed the Universal Declaration of Human Rights in 1948 and has created over 80 treaties since. Presently, 47,650 UN troops and personnel are in more than 80 countries to maintain peace, set up treaties and protect human rights. The UN and its agencies provide about $30 billion a year in aid. They provide one third of the food aid in the world, immunize three million children a year and provide one billion a year in emergency aid.

- *The International Red Cross* is a humanitarian organization that was originally founded "to preserve a measure of humanity in the face of war. We believe that even in war there are limits on how warfare is conducted and limits on how combatants behave." The set of rules that was established under this philosophy was endorsed by almost every nation in the world and called the International Humanitarian Law. Later this would build the Geneva Conventions. In 1859, a man named Henri Dunant, a Swiss citizen, passed through a town in Italy where a bitter battle was taking place between the Austrian and French armies. He was horrified by the sight of thousands of soldiers left to suffer without any medical care. He appealed to the local people to help tend to the wounded, insisting that soldiers on both sides should be cared for equally. When he returned to Switzerland he published this story and appealed for relief societies to be formed during peacetime with nurses that would be ready to care for the wounded in wartime and that these volunteers would be recognized and protected through an international agreement. So began the Red Cross. They state they have one purpose: to maintain, support and respect the International Humanitarian Law. This organization now has a huge agenda including landmines, war and displacement assistance, finding missing children, war and money, children as soldiers and humanitarian debates. Their home is in Geneva, but they are in over 80 countries.

- *Doctors Without Borders* is an organization that delivers emergency aid to victims of armed conflicts, epidemics, natural and man-made disasters and to others who lack needed healthcare due to their social or geographical status.

This was founded in 1971 by a group of French doctors who believe "that all people have the right to medical care, regardless of race, religion, creed or political affiliation, and that the needs of these people superseded respect for national borders."

This is a private non-profit organization (the first to give medical assistance and hear the plight of people) that gives medical care including surgery, trains local doctors, builds hospitals and rehab centers, sets up nutrition and sanitation programs and creates mental health programs.

They are dedicated to providing not only medical care, but becoming "witnesses to, and speaking out against, the underlying causes behind the suffering of humanity." Each year more than 2,500 volunteer doctors, nurses, other medical staff, administration assistants, logistical experts and water/sanitation engineers join the over 15,000 locally hired staff in over 80 countries. You do not have to have a medical background to work with this organization, but you are required to go through training and must commit to a minimum of six months, more often one to three years. They will take on specialty people like surgeons for emergent cases lasting only a few months.

- *The Nobel Peace Prize* is a humanitarian award given out yearly, along with a substantial monetary award, to the person or organization that was considered to have contributed in a large way something that affected humanity in a positive way. Alfred Nobel (1833-1896) was born in Sweden but raised in Russia. He was well educated by private tutors. As an adult, he was an inventor, writer, scientist and humanitarian. In his lifetime he held over 350 patents on all the different things he invented or created, including dynamite. He also wrote poetry, painted and was considering becoming a playwright. A year before he died, he set up a foundation to give international recognition and financial assistance to people or groups (consisting of no more than three individuals) who contributed something to humanity that was significant in helping the world evolve. He divided his grants into five categories: medicine, physics, literature, economics and humanitarianism, which he called the Nobel Peace Prize. The first four categories had a foundation set up in Sweden to research, evaluate, submit and choose the recipient for each year. The Nobel Peace Prize foundation was given to Norway and they set up their own independent committee that consists of six people who are voted into "office" and have a rather complex system to maintain the neutrality and integrity of the process. Mr. Nobel never explained why he separated out the Peace Prize from the other four categories or why he endowed it to another country. He spent the last year of his life carefully setting up the foundation with many attorneys and government officials to ensure that it would be implemented as he envisioned it. Soon after signing over the foundations, he quietly died of "some sort of brain bleed."

MIDDLE EAST

- *Israel/Palestine* The land that is now called Israel has a long history of being tied to the Jewish culture. Throughout thousands of years this area was overtaken by multiple people, often going east to west or west to east for wars, but historically Arabs lived in this territory, specifically the Palestinians. The Jewish people were often enslaved by the various peoples as they temporarily occupied the land. After WWI, many land boundaries all over Europe and the Middle East were re-written (which often happens after a war), with new countries being formed. At this time Great Britain had agreements with the Arabs, but they also had relations with the Jewish community, but to uphold an Arab agreement they did stop Jewish influx into the Palestinian area for a while. After WWII (when over six million Jews were purposefully killed), the UN partitioned land for them and Israel was formally born. There are reports that the U.S. heavily influenced the formation of Israel, which the American government denies, but the supposed tight relationship between the U.S. and Israel is a cause of anger and resentment among some in the Arab world. The Palestinians, who throughout their history fought hard for their land, were not in agreement with the UN's decision. Between 1947, the formal inception of Israel, and 1967, there were several serious conflicts between the Arabs of Palestine and the Jewish settlers of Israel. In 1967, there was a "Six-Day War" that was very violent. The Jewish community was upset that the U.S. did not back them, but they did an amazing job of holding back the Arab population which was much, much larger than theirs. After this very bloody and harsh period, the Jewish settlers were given two pieces of land: the Gaza Strip and the West Bank. More importantly to them, they won the city of Jerusalem from Jordan, a neighboring Arab country, which is a city considered very holy in the Jewish religion, Christianity and Islam. The Islamic Arab culture was not accepting of this loss. The Palestinians, under the ruler Yasser Arafat, created the PLO (Palestinian Liberation Movement), which was accused of being a terrorist group. In 1988, the PLO and Israel came to a peace agreement that created a two-party state. This would be like the U.S. state of Illinois having the central city of Champaign and the larger city of Chicago considered a separate state with a separate government within the overall state of Illinois. Despite this agreement, violence continued between the Palestinians and the Jewish settlers. Thousands were killed on both sides, especially through suicide bombers. But in 1992, representatives from both countries met secretly in Norway and, working with Norwegian mediators, came to an agreement. They developed what they called a "Framework for Peace" instead of a solution. When they publicly announced this everyone was surprised, especially the U.S. and the UN, who had no idea this was going on. Right after this, the PLO renounced violence, but splinter groups continued with the violence and the Israel Defense Forces (IDF) also continued with some violence. By 2000, both sides were openly fighting again. There are many more complex layers to this issue, including conflicts with neighboring countries and new groups which some label "terrorist groups" like Hamas, which had members that actually became elected Palestinian officials after spending years fighting Israel. This makes peace between the two states an even more complex issue. Also, there are the very strong cultural and religious ties both parties have to the land, both believing that God intended them to live there. Religious fervor, years of oppression and generations of violence between the Islamic Arabs and Israeli Jews have built a foundation of distrust and hatred that will have to be dissolved before moving forward in a more permanent state of peaceful resolutions and living cohesively together.

• *NATO* (North Atlantic Treaty Organization) was founded in 1949 (after WWII) and is dedicated to "safeguard the freedom of peoples... principles of democracy... and stability in North America." Headquartered in Brussels, there are 26 member countries in Europe and North America who state that they are united to preserve peace. The countries involved in NATO have complex agreements among them, including military agreements, which have been tested many times when the countries have fundamentally disagreed about how to handle certain conflicts. From the late 1940s until the early 1990s, the U.S. and USSR were engaged in what was called "the Cold War," fighting against each other through other countries and situations. There were some very tenuous and dangerous times during this period, challenging the NATO principles which the U.S. was part of (though not initially, Europe didn't want U.S. participation) and the USSR was not. They did request a place in NATO, but were not accepted.

Change

Change is a process; it takes time. There are no sweeping solutions to problems, no easy outs to things that have been building for years, and absolutely no way to just make everything go away. Some part in everyone, an aspect of their ego, wants this. It wants simple solutions that just make problems go away.

Life is a learning process, but we only learn if we face the mistakes we've made. We need to face our messes because we often learn the most in life by cleaning up those messes. Most people are pretty defended against admitting to their personal mistakes, let alone owning up to choices they make that detrimentally affect the world on a global level, like driving personal vehicles that get low gas mileage.

No crisis happens overnight, crises happen because people don't deal with things that aren't working out along the way. It's like personal debt; people often let it build and build without facing and dealing with it until it becomes a personal crisis for them. But that crisis built up over a long period of time. And it's not going away overnight.

Part of the process of growth is evaluation, and when you honestly go back and evaluate something you have to face what worked and what didn't. Then you have to be willing to humbly own up to what didn't work and change it, not deny that it was your fault or make excuses. Try making different choices instead, do different things, open yourself up to a different perspective and genuinely learn to be a different way in the

25

world.

As a whole, humanity will not move forward if we don't face the mistakes we've made and do something about them. Why are there still wars? How can half the world be living in poverty? How can there be so many dictators (over fifty) that rule over countries in some pretty harsh ways? How can 36,000 people a day die as a result of poverty in a world that has a "billionaires" club? How can people starve to death by the millions each year? These are problems that have been around for many generations. Are we going to be the generation that starts to reverse the process?

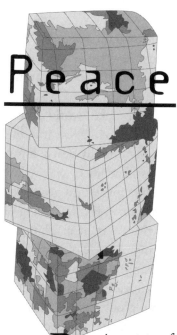

Peace

Peace is a state of <u>inner</u> calm; it actually has nothing to do with what's going on around you. The world can be in great turmoil and you can still be in peace. It's a bit unrealistic to ask for world peace, because group dynamics change one person at a time, not as a whole group. Group mentality can appear to change on the surface, but it's actually just a façade. In other words, people will just blindly follow something in a group without really understanding what's going on, but they'll usually only do that for a little while and then go back to how things were. Real change is an in-depth process that requires things like facing your mistakes, dealing with problems, a willingness to fluidly change, letting go of control and seeing a larger picture than just what's going on in this moment of your life. Peace is found one person at a time, not in a group, by each person finding their place in the world and owning up to their life choices. This planet has over six and a half billion people on it, so it's very unrealistic to think that all those people, who have vastly different cultural beliefs and philosophies, are going to come together and be peaceful as one group. People find peace as individuals, not as a whole.

Peace really is a state of personal inner calm and is achieved by learning to accept the reality of both yourself and what's going on around you, even if it's not pleasant. **Having things be "nice" and being at peace have nothing to do with one another.** Peace is a state of inner acceptance, and from there you can make choices and take actions to change what isn't working. You have to accept what is, no matter how unpleasant, before you can change anything. Otherwise you're just reacting to something you don't like, and reactionary behavior doesn't change anything long-term (and often causes more harm).

When people make statements about things like "world peace," what they're usually saying is that they want all the violence, war and conflicts to end in the world. Technically, that's not actually peace; it just means people aren't overtly fighting, but there's still conflict. They're just fighting in a different way. People have been calling for "world peace" for I don't know how long, but it's been a really long time. If it was going to happen, it would have. What I'm saying here is that we've been asking for the wrong thing. Peace is a personal state of mind, or state of being. Just because there isn't a war or overt violence does not mean there's peace. Plenty of science fiction books and movies have dealt with this concept by depicting societies living in a state of overall group polite calmness, with no outward conflict only to find out they're all drugged up or programmed, or some such thing. It is childlike and naïve to think billions of people can share a planet and not have conflict. Conflict does not have to escalate to violence, but it will exist.

Going after world peace is not about going after things like trying to get all people to give up arms and get along. There are presently too many variables for that to happen, too many differences in people, including maturity levels. Trying to formulate national policies or solutions to get millions of people to behave a certain way doesn't work. It's been tried for decades, unsuccessfully. You can only force a society to comply for so long. Peace is an event that happens when one person at a time becomes more aware, more culturally connected, more globally connected and then personally responsible.

You cannot "make" anyone "get" anything. People understand at their own pace and in their own timing. It doesn't mean you shouldn't try and help people see the bigger picture that goes on in the world, or challenge them to face their part in society and in life. I do it virtually every day, trying to help bring more awareness to people, but bringing awareness to people and trying to force them to "get it" is crossing the line between allowing people to have their own personal thoughts and understandings of the information coming their way, and trying to force them to believe and think exactly as you do.

Peace is attainable in the world, just not throughout the world the way most people think about it. Stopping conflicts and finding peace are two completely different things. Peace is you finding yourself and your place in the world; it is not about stopping violence. Governments could overtake their people and forcibly stop violence (ironically through violence), but that does not bring peace to the land. The more individual people mature and find their own inner peace, the more outer peace will be achieved in this world. Acting peaceful and being in a state of inner peace is not the same thing. The first one is easily taunted back into violence under high pressured conditions, and the second one is not. It will remain peaceful no matter the circumstances.

Evolution

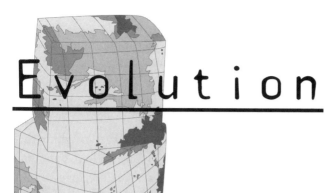

E volution is a process of growth where you actually move on to another level of Being in the world. It's not just about learning to do something new. It's actually learning to become a whole new person in the world. It's like someone who was an alcoholic who treated people terribly when they were drinking and caused a lot of harm. Then they go through some kind of personal situation or transformation and sober up. In time, after they work out their personal issues that they drank to avoid, plus take ownership for harm they caused, they find not only a new state of inner peace but also see the world differently. From here they treat other people differently, with depth and a higher tolerance for people and their issues. They're different now because they've been through something and have gotten to the other side. They really understand inner conflict and denial, and the process of taking issues out on other people. They're not just acting nice, they've become more tolerant, understanding and compassionate. They have now evolved to another level of Being, another level of personal maturity.

Evolution, just like peace, happens one person at a time. Life is not just there, it really is a learning background for growth and evolution. The more you get out in the world and understand yourself and what's going on, the more you change, grow and evolve. The more you turn off the news, develop an attitude where you don't want to deal with anything and live half or more of your day in denial, the less and less evolved you become. Yes, people actually become less evolved during their life. Look around at how many people you know that are less aware, seem less intelligent and less present than they did years ago. We're all energy in this world, and energy is always in motion, so you're either moving forward in life or moving back. No one stands still.

Evolution is a choice. You have to choose not to get caught in that place where you only see the negative, or bad, in change. Where you think every new piece of technology is ridiculous or a waste of time, for example. You have to choose to live your life with an open mind. You also have to choose to move forward emotionally. You have to choose to mature to a level where life isn't just about getting your personal needs met, or being supported by others, being popular, making money or gaining status in the world. We're coming to a dangerous place in time where there is so much evolution happening on certain levels, like interconnectedness and information, yet personal evolution is being stunted by personal ego. In a state of emotional maturity, your "wants" do not always come first. The next level in mankind's overall evolution is globalization, finding harmony and connection throughout the world. This requires people to gain enough personal emotional maturity that their ego-based desires, like looking pretty and shopping as a sport, do not take precedent over that which affects everyone else. When you put things like your personal appearance above things like recycling and health, then you're choosing to go backwards in evolution instead of forward.

I'm not saying people shouldn't shop or care about their appearance, but caring about your appearance and crossing over the line into vanity, which will dominate many other things in life, is an issue that eventually becomes a global problem. When you spend more time on the Internet playing with your "profile" and your "picture" and how many "friends" you have instead of understanding what's happening in today's news, economy, politics, healthcare and so on, you are going backwards, not forward.

Evolution is a process of maturity, and maturity requires that you let go of your rationales and defenses to deal with things as they are. To see things as they are. For example, I have heard so many women and, sadly, girls state that they aren't "vain," they just want to get their breasts surgically enlarged so they can feel better about themselves. That is vanity. You can sugarcoat it any way you want, but that's vanity. Lying to yourself is one of the ego's greatest pastimes, and it keeps you in an immature state. Immaturity keeps you from evolving, and lack of evolution means you stay stuck in life. The more people get stuck, no matter how sophisticated their ego makes it look, the less humanity as a whole will move forward to a more mature way of being with each other. Without this growth in maturity and evolution, there really will never be peace in this world.

We really do evolve one person at a time. Face the lies you tell yourself, and then face the lies you read and hear in the world. Face the truth about what's going on, mature to your highest capability and live the life you were literally born to live in this world.

Globalization

This word means many things to many people, but right now in our history it's basically the connection of humanity on the planet. This involves the interconnection of things like technology, governing bodies, corporations, health and education organizations and financial institutions. It also involves people being more tolerant and compassionate, understanding how other governments work (understanding the reality of how your government works!), understanding the media process, the education process and so much more. It requires that you get your mind out of the small box it lives in and learn to see the world from other people's points of view. Your way in this world is not the "right way," it's just your way. Understanding how other people see the world, what others think and believe is essential to our evolution if it's going to be a healthy one.

Globalization isn't just something like the Internet itself being connected all around the world. It also involves *how* people use the Internet. Globalization is a potentially dangerous thing because there's a lot of advanced technology that goes along with it, but technology does not evolve people, people evolve themselves by maturing to the next level within them. If people don't mature as advancing technology becomes more and more globally available, it becomes a dangerous situation.

Part of your maturing process is learning to work with things like advanced technology, to be aware of what's going on in the world, and to understand your personal responsibility in the world, which includes seeing a bigger picture of how things both connect and work in this world. You want the world to be a better place, less violent, less judgmental and less harsh? Then start with yourself becoming more aware and involved in the world. Most violence, prejudice and judgment in the world comes out of ignorance, and ignorance comes from going through life unaware. For example, a person goes to their local grocery store and finds the major thing they wanted, let's say milk, isn't in stock. Then they have a knee-jerk angry reaction at the store and everyone working there because their normal routine, picking up milk on Fridays was interrupted. But there was a terrible storm the day before and the truck driver can't safely get through until later on today. People often don't put these things together. No matter what the weather, or any other dangerous situation going on, people expect their personal routines in this country to stay the same, and they can get pretty angry when that doesn't happen. Ultimately that anger is coming out of a lack of connection and awareness. They aren't connecting to what's really going on around them, the severity of the weather in this case, and they aren't aware of the difficulty and skill level in driving a semi-truck through harsh weather. Often people are only aware of their personal routines in life.

When you don't have a deeper understanding about what's going on, whether it's because you're not aware or because you don't want to get out of your limited way of thinking, you're more likely to be very judgmental and prejudiced toward others. It's like people who have never been fifty or more pounds overweight who easily think, "they should eat less," or "why don't they just lose some weight," when they see someone who is very overweight in their opinion. Don't fool yourself. When you do things like this, you're silently judging and attacking someone based on, in this case their weight, with no understanding of what they're going through. You're not deeply aware of what's really happening, so your perceptions and responses are both superficial and harsh. Another common example is someone who has never loved a pet not understanding why someone who just lost theirs is so upset. To them, the person is just being overly dramatic.

Globalization is a very mature place to be if you're going to be successful at it. You have to become aware of life outside the way you see things and the experiences you've had. It also takes a willingness to participate in things that may serve a purpose beyond what you can immediately see, or that serves someone other than yourself. For example, many Americans complain about jobs being outsourced to other countries. I realize this is a very sensitive topic for many people, but on a mature level of economic globalization, outsourcing jobs to other countries can be a very globally humane thing to do if our economy is stable because it can give people elsewhere a place to grow and evolve. In this country the majority of people have evolved or matured to a place where they are capable of doing more than they do. For example, many families talk about being "fifth generation" to work at a specific factory, as if that's a good thing. There is absolutely nothing wrong with working in a factory, but for five generations of one family to be doing the same job can indicate a lack of evolution. When factories close their doors, maybe it's a sign to move on to something else completely, to challenge yourself to learn and grow in something totally new. I realize this can really anger some people, but life is a teacher, and in the teaching process we are often challenged by some harsh situations to change and move on. People are forced to do this all the time after severe accidents or life threatening diseases. They use those experiences to propel them out in the world to learn and do something else with their lives. They often don't have a choice. The loss of a job source can do the same thing; open people's minds up to a new way of being in the world.

In many third world countries, people live a farming life or something similar that is often family-related but does not require many personal skills, like showing up "9 to 5" someplace routinely, learning to communicate on a business level, learning to interact with people outside their village/family/community, learning to earn specific wages and deal with things like work reviews, schedules and expectations. They are also not used to earning their own money and all the responsibility that entails. For them, working in a factory job is an important part in the next level of their personal evolvement. Their country doesn't have an economy that could open a factory, but they can host one, like a company from the U.S.

Simply put, when you evolve to a level where you can meet your own basic needs, there is a natural process where you turn around and help other people. It's part of the maturing process. It's like a stable company hiring a certain number of people in transition to help them either grow or get back on track. It's the humanitarian thing to do. And globally, when a country reaches a certain level of sustainability, it now has an obligation to turn around and help others outside that country to give them an opportunity to grow beyond where they might be stuck or suffering. In order for this mature level of globalization to work, the individuals in that country have to be mature enough to want to help people outside their country (if their country's economy is stable). They have to want to be aware of just how hard others have it and how inhumane it is not to offer help.

Many will read this and say some version of, "But we have too many problems in this country to be putting our money and job opportunities in other countries," and they'd be right. At this time, we really do, but as much as people might not want to hear this, much of our economic distress is due to things like people not wanting to move on and making too many financial choices based in ego (buying that overly large house, multiple expensive televisions, etc.) instead of slowing down and being aware of what's going on around you, which can help you make healthier choices. It's become a phenomenon in America how many people are financially stressed, yet still overspend. Then they become angry when they lose their job, can't sell their house or get a loan because they aren't paying attention to the overall economy, the housing market or their job environment. They want to be bailed out for their bad choices.

It's a very immature place to be when you think that you should only live for yourself, only spend money on yourself, keep all jobs and revenue that flows through this country in this country forever. We are part of the world, and the world is part of us. Knowing what's going on in the world is part of your job as an adult, and so is being mature enough to give other people an opportunity to grow. Is global economics working as great as it could? Absolutely not; there are a ton of problems including abuse, but very few things in history ever worked out great when they first started out. And maybe it's not going to. Maybe humanity isn't mature enough yet to share. Maybe we all have more growing to do before globalization will be successful. Time will show us the results, but for now, how willing are you to become more aware? If you have financial investments, do you understand what you're invested in? Do you know what a Socially Conscious Fund is? The U.S. is run by its economy, but do you understand how the economy works? Can you name your state senator(s) and representatives? Can you explain how congress works, sub-committees and lobbyists? Are you willing to personally research all of this and more so that you can understand your world? Are you willing to be more mature, to grow up and share? Because things like sharing, seeing the world from a larger perspective, seeing your choices and situation from a larger perspective, and not always having everything about you and getting what you want is a major part in the next level of maturity and evolution. Are you ready? Because the world in which you live is already going there.

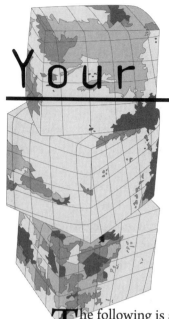

Your World

The following is a list of the present countries and territories that exist. It is a very brief and **generalized** description, as again my intention is to bring the reader awareness, not fill them with technical information. There really is a difference.

You are not alone in this world; you share this planet with literally billions of other people. On some level, what you do affects them and what they do affects you. There are hundreds of other countries, over a dozen religions, over fifty languages, hundreds of different cultures, more than twenty different types of governments and so forth. There are a lot of other perspectives and experiences in life than just yours. Connection is not about bringing your way of doing things and your thoughts to someone else in order to get them to follow "your way." It's about explaining your perspectives and learning to understand theirs, and then working with both together. Changing the world does not mean changing people to your way of being. It's a big world, so you might want to challenge the smallness of your life with the bigness of what's going on out there. How do you fit into the world? Maybe it's time you found out.

Afghanistan, *1919*

They have a long history of both civil wars and external wars without any real independent government formed. The country originated in 1747, was taken over by Britain and gained independence in 1919. The people here believe the land is holy. The Taliban originated here while the

41

country was busy keeping itself divided into four different sections. There is no real economy, there are poor land resources and the whole country is in poverty. After 9/11, there were large donations of money made to this country by U.S. citizens after learning of their plight and oppression by the Taliban. The money is being held by the World Bank (millions) until an infrastructure is established. Though they now have a government, the country is still impoverished and lives daily with U.S. and coalition armies fighting the Taliban. The people themselves live hard lives, claiming that at least when the Taliban was in power they generally had daily peace, even though they were run by a militia group, compared to their lives since 9/11 which have been filled with daily unrest and violence. They are also struggling with maturing to a formal government system.

Akrotiri and Dhekeli

This is actually a 254-kilometer piece of land inside of Cypress that Britain still holds as part of their territories. It houses an airbase for the British military.

Albania, 1912

In 1990, this country ended 44 years of hardcore communistic rule and have been working toward becoming a democratic society ever since. They have a poor economy, poverty, poor education and a weak infrastructure due to "gangster-like" groups that controlled a fledgling government until 2005, when a Democratic Party was elected. They cleaned up the gang problem and got this country turned around. They are working toward entry into the EU and NATO. Though a very small country, they have done a strong job in dealing with inter-ethnic issues (they used to be divided into 36 sections) and participate heavily in European issues.

Algeria, 1962

This country just recently got its independence from France, but was run by the Islamic army until 2000. In the 1990's, they had over 100,000 deaths due to insurgency. It has the 5th largest natural resources on the planet (especially in petroleum), but its people are poorly educated and the money is not distributed. The country is working on becoming socialist but is plagued with infighting with its own army.

American Samoa

In 1899, Germany owned the Samoan Islands. They sold a small portion to the U.S. The U.S. uses the harbor of Pago Pago for military purposes.

Andorra, *1278*

This country sits between France and Spain. Prior to WWII it was very impoverished and isolated because of the mountainous region. It now does well because of tourism, which is 90% of their economy. They have no income tax, which attracts a lot of immigrants.

Angola, *1975*

This country sits on oil but has been involved in civil war since inception, so its resources have never been fully realized. The country has a 300% inflation rate and is very poverty oriented. They separated from Portugal in 1975, but never established their own government and have been in civil war ever since. They have lost an estimated 1.5 million people due to civil war between 1992 and 2002. Civil war ended in 2002. The country claims they will hold elections (for the first time) in 2008.

Antigua and Barbuda, *1981*

These are independent states of the Commonwealth of Britain since 1981. They have been natively inhabited since 2400 BC. They have also taken on over 3,000 refugees from nearby islands, mainly due to volcanic eruptions. Tourism is their main income. They have a chronic water problem and apathy from the general population to develop their own natural farming resources.

Argentina, *1816*

From 1976 to 1983, this country was under military rule, but then a democratic leader took over. The country has many natural resources and the people are well-educated, but the government in the late 80s largely overspent and imported much of what the country already had, plunging the country into economic failure with a 200% inflation rate. They went through several interim leaders, and in 2001 the country was in an economic crisis where the public had many violent protests. In 2002 a more stable government was founded, and by 2006 most of its debt to the IMF was paid off and the economy began to stabilize.

Armenia, *1991*

They became independent of USSR in 1991. They claim to be the first nation to adopt Christianity in the early 4th century. Since 1988 they have been fighting their neighboring state (Muslim), Azerbaijan, and the war intensified when both states became independent in 1991. A cease-fire has been in existence since 1994 (they fought over land rights and religion). They are fighting over neighboring Nagorno-Karabakh, which is mainly occupied by Armenians but disputed by Muslim Azerbaijan. Turkey has put economic blockades on Armenia as a way of protesting their dispute. Armenia has worked hard to educate its people, set up small business sectors and become involved internationally. They sought international help for growth in their infrastructure, and because of this, they have done very well.

Arctic Ocean

This is the smallest of the world's five oceans but it holds two of the world's most important seasonal waterways. Its ownership is disputed by many countries. No indigenous peoples live here, but multiple countries desire to own it because of the petroleum, natural gas, fish and seals.

Aruba, *1499*

This Caribbean island was founded by Spain and then taken over by the Dutch and eventually became part of the Netherlands. In the 19th century there was a huge gold rush that brought a lot of prosperity to the island. In 1924 they opened an oil refinery. In recent years tourism has become big, although they have had some problems with hurricanes. The Netherlands were moving this island toward independence in 1990 when Aruba halted the process. They are recognized as a separate but autonomous part of the Netherlands.

Ashmore and Cartier Islands, *1931*

This is a small set of uninhabitable islands next to Australia. It has a very rich marine habitat, and a National Nature Reserve was created here. The environment is now protected, but ironically it is a former bombing range.

Atlantic Ocean

This is the second largest of the world's five oceans. In the year 2000 the International Hydrographic Organization redefined its perimeters, removing a large portion and calling it South Atlantic Ocean. Its waterways are used by most countries. It holds large icebergs and its resources include oil, gas, fish and marine animals.

Australia, *1901*

Australia has been a Commonwealth of Britain since 1901 (originally colonized as an island prison) and has tried to become independent ever since without success (last attempt 1999). Their economy is very similar to that of the U.S., and follows about six months behind it.

Austria, *1955*

Once part of Hungary (and very powerful, known as the Austro-Hungarian Empire), this country fell after WWI and then again after WWII. They created independence in 1955 with the help of the international community because Russia fought against giving them independence, demanding that they sign a declaration that they could not unify with Germany. There was a lot of bitterness between these two countries after WWII. Today they are financially powerful, well-educated and strong in the European Union. The country is only 2% indigenous, 80% German. The rest of the population includes Slavs, Croats and Romanians.

Azerbaijan, *1991*

This country separated from Russia in 1991 and has been fighting with its neighbor Armenia since 1988. They have been in a cease-fire since 1994, but are unstable in their peace. The war is over land; Armenia wants the Nagorno-Karabakh area (mostly populated by Armenians). This country sits on oil, but the government is corrupt and the people do not see the money. They have over 750,000 refugees living on the land. The people are very impoverished, and the infrastructure is underdeveloped.

Bahamas, *1973*

This Caribbean island became independent of Britain in 1973 and has prospered through tourism, but they have a huge problem with drug smuggling (mostly to the U.S.). Because of this, there is a huge problem with violent crime, which is now affecting their tourism trade. They also hold offshore bank accounts for people.

Bahrain, *1971*

They became independent of Britain in 1971 and their economy is based on oil refinery (they have minimal oil themselves). Originally, the Al Khalifa family captured this country from Persia and made a deal with Britain, which is how they came to be under British rule for so long. They sit in the Persian Gulf and have precarious relationships because the Middle East is their income for oil to refine, with the U.S. and Europe as their buyers. There was great strife within the Shia community, so in 1999 the King (newly in power) pushed a lot of reforms, and the Shia community came into power in Parliament and municipal elections. In the last two years, Shia "discontent" has resurfaced and people are demonstrating in the streets with low-level violence for now.

Baker Island, *1857*

The U.S. took possession of this island and worked with the British in the early 19th century mining its minerals. In 1935, there was an attempt to inhabit the island that was stopped by WWII and never tried again due to conditions on the island. Today it is considered a natural wildlife refuge and the U.S. military has equipment on the island.

Bangladesh, *1971*

They seceded from Pakistan in 1971. Initially India was one country, then Pakistan and East Bengal (both Muslim) separated off from Hindu-based India after India became independent of Britain. East Bengal became East Pakistan, but the union was never stable and it separated off in 1971, becoming their own country of Bangladesh. About one third of the country is wiped out every year from flooding. Two thirds of the country's population works in rice fields. The country is extremely poor and extremely over-populated. They have had enormous help from outside the country but it refuses to change. They are gridlocked in old world cultures and a constantly changing and corrupt government. They want aid but they refuse to change.

Barbados, *1966*

The British discovered this island uninhabited in 1627 and it became part of their Commonwealth until 1966 when it gained independence. They traditionally have had a strong economy based on rum and sugar. In the 1990s the tourism trade brought in more than their sugar and rum exports. They also deal with offshore accounts.

Bassas da India, *1897*

This is a volcanic rock that is outside of Southern Africa. It sits between Madagascar and Mozambique. It is unlivable and uninhabitable and Madagascar is disputing it.

Belarus, *1991*

After 24 years of fighting, they gained independence from Russia in 1991. The country maintains strong ties with Russia, especially economic. The current president is very aggressive and treats the country much like a communistic state, oppresses the people, no religious freedom, raids on business, etc. They have a poor economy at this time.

Belgium, *1830*

This country separated off from the Netherlands and was occupied both in WWI and WWII. It has strong technological strengths and is a prominent member of NATO. The north speaks Dutch and the south speaks French. They have been divided in culture as well; in the last several years, it has been so bad that their constitution has been amended several times to recognize autonomy to both areas.

Belize, *1981*

This country used to be called British Honduras; part Britain-owned and part Guatemala. They finally got their independence in 1981, but only in 1992 did Guatemala acknowledge it. They are extremely poor and tourism is their only real economy, but drug trafficking and mob-like violence is a constant problem. They also have a huge problem with chronic hurricanes.

Benin, *1960*

This country used to be called Dahomey and is in (west) Africa. It became independent of France in 1960 and changed its name in 1975. It took on a socialist government from 1974 to 1989. They became a free republic in 1991 and held their first elections. This is an underdeveloped country that relies on cotton and local trade but has a problem with AIDS. It has become more stable over the last five years and is trying to attract tourism and outside trading.

Bermuda, *1609*

This island was discovered by English colonists who got shipwrecked on the way to Virginia and ended up colonizing the island. Its major economy today is offshore banking and tourism. International business and banking is its largest income. It attempted independence in 1995 from Britain but was unsuccessful.

Bhutan, *1949*

This country sits between China and India. In the 1800s, it joined with the Commonwealth of Britain for protection and trade. In 1947, it split off, signing treaties for India to rule its internal affairs, and Britain its external affairs. In 1949, they separated from India but have a complex treaty with them. There are more than 100,000 Bhutanese refugees in Nepal (living in UN housing) because of discrepancies with India. They had never developed their own constitution until 2005, when the ruling King introduced democratic reforms and pledged to hold national referendums. To date, nothing has changed or come into formal ruling. This is potentially the most undeveloped country at this time.

Bolivia, *1825*

This country has had over 200 coups and is the least developed Latin American country. They became a democratic country in 1980. Their economy and stability picked up from 1993 to 1999 because the (then) president created mass internal growth and stability. Since the current president has taken over, the country has started having brutal civil unrests since 2000. The country is split between two major cultures, the non-indigenous people in the lowlands, and the Amerindian population of the Andean west. There is a huge split between these two peoples economically and in how they want the country run. They also have a large drug trade.

Bosnia-Herzegovina, *1991*

This country recently came out of a brutal civil war to declare its independence from Yugoslavia. The war was based on ethnicity. Neighboring Serbia wanted the country (Yugoslavia) to be turned into all Serbs (calling it a Greater Serbia), and Serbs living within Bosnia joined in attacking their fellow countryman. Yugoslavia broke apart into multiple regions, one being Croatia, a neighbor to Bosnia. In 1994, at the height of the war, Bosnia and Croatia joined together signing a peace deal (brokered by Jimmy Carter). The deal created a very complex three-tiered government. NATO kept troops in the country to prevent further violence until 2004, and then European Union peacekeepers took over until 2007. Many of the people are still refugees living outside the country.

Botswana, *1966*

The country became independent of Britain in 1966 and has a strong economy in diamond mining. This used to be the poorest country. It has the highest growth rate of any country since its independence, but they have a problem with unemployment, education and AIDS.

Boubet Island, *1739*

This is an uninhabited volcanic island that is covered by glaciers and is difficult to access. The French discovered it, gave it to Britain, and in 1928 Britain gave it to Norway. Norway monitors the volcanic activity.

Brazil, *1822*

This is the largest country in South America and they spent over 60 years in military internal warring. In 1985 the military quietly gave over power to the civilian government. They have been very industrialized and profitable since the 1970s, but they have a huge discrimination in salaries. They're either really wealthy or really poor, which creates an unstable populace. They currently have a large problem with inflation and owe a lot of money to outside sources. They have vast resources and a large labor pool creating South America's leading economic country for the past several years. AIDS is fast on the rise.

British Indian Ocean Territory, *1965*

This is a series of small islands in the Indian Ocean just south of India. Britain claimed the islands but technically there is a U.S. partnership. The U.S. wanted Chagos Island for military use. The island was populated with 1,200 people. Since it was illegal to force these people off the island, through the technicality of calling indigenous people "agricultural workers," they were forced off the island by the U.S. military. The island's name was changed to Diego Garcia. 3,500 UK and U.S. military people, along with some civilians, have occupied the island for the last 30 years. Many of the indigenous people died as a result of poverty as they were put into slums on a neighboring island. These people had previously been prosperous, healthy and living in their own homes. An international rights group from Britain has spent over 20 years going after the U.S. and UK government for their inhumane and illegal treatment of the Chagos people.

British Virgin Islands, *1648*

These islands were founded by the Dutch and handed over to the British. They sit right next to the U.S. Virgin Islands, so they follow U.S. economy, including U.S. dollar. The area remains a territory of Britain and is one of the most stable and prosperous in the Caribbean. The majority of tourists come from the U.S., which accounts for 50% of its income. In 1994 there was an insurance law adopted that provides "blanket of confidentiality," so by 2000 there were over 400,000 companies listed in their offshore banking accounts.

Brunei, *1984*

This country is by the Philippines and has been under the same family rule for six centuries. They have oil, but no well-developed refineries. They spent a few hundred years in civil wars and still have problems with internal fighting and piracy (they are an island). They declared independence from the Commonwealth of Britain in 1984.

Bulgaria, *1878*

This country has a history of being ruled by many other countries, including Russia, until its political independence in 1991. It now functions as a fledgling democratic society (since 1994) and is struggling with poverty, poor economy and inflation. It joined the European Union and NATO by 2007. This country has reached a place where they experience 5% growth per year (since 2000). Minerals are their major economy, and recently, outside investments.

Burkina Faso, *1960*

This country in West Africa became independent from France in 1960, but has struggled with many, many governmental bodies since. They are one of the poorest countries in the world. They are focused on agriculture, but their soil is very poor. They are dying of AIDS. Now they seek to establish some kind of economic system in industry. Unrest in neighboring Cote d'Ivoire and Ghana are causing unrest in this country.

Burma, *1962*

This country in Asia has been under constant military aggression. Initially Britain spent 62 years fighting to get this land and then incorporated it into India. Britain developed what it called the Indian Empire back in the late 1800s. Republic elections were held in 1990, but the military (called the Junta) has maintained control and refuses to acknowledge the government. Nobel Peace Prize recipient Aung San Suu Kyi has been under house arrest since 1989 for trying to bring democracy to the country. They are resource-rich, but live in poverty and isolation. Information is limited coming in and out of Burma. The military is aggressive and isolating. The people here are routinely tortured and abused, teachers routinely killed.

Burundi, *1962*

Burundi became a formal country in 1962 (previously held by Belgium). This country sits next to Rwanda, a country torn apart by civil war between two cultures: the Hutus and the Tutsis. Both of these cultures have spilled over into Burundi. In 1993 the first democratically elected President was assassinated after 100 days in office, triggering widespread violence between the Hutus and the Tutsis living here. Over 200,000 people were slaughtered, and hundreds of thousands of Burundis were displaced in this continued conflict between the Rwanda Hutu and Tutsi factions. The government was overtaken by the Tutsis. In 2003, a deal was brokered between the Hutus and the Tutsis, and a new constitution was developed in 2004. The government is Hutu majority at this time. The country is still unstable. They have very few indigenous resources, are landlocked, and their major export is coffee.

Cambodia, *1953*

This country was involved in a violent civil uprising in 1975, and approximately 1.5 million people were tortured to death by the Khmer Rouge army under Pol Pot. Most Cambodians consider themselves to be "Khmer," who are descendents of the Angkor Empire from the 10th-13th centuries. This was especially gruesome in that Pol Pot stole most of the children in the nation and brainwashed/tortured them into believing their parents were evil, so much of the killing and capturing (often of their own family) was done by the children. Although child soldiers still exist all over the world, this was one of the worst cases of brainwashing and using children in combat ever seen. This regime was known for its extremeness; for example, there was a hall leading into an area where individual torture took place. The people who were doing the torture had their pictures on the wall and they actually had a "torturer of the week" contest where the winner's picture was put in first place. To win, you had to inflict the most torture without killing the victim too soon. Whoever could torture someone the longest won for that week. In 1978, the Vietnamese invaded and they fought in the country for 13 years, driving the Khmer Rouge out. In 1993, the UN helped them establish a coalition government, but the country was ravaged and wounded. The country fell into in-fighting in 1997, and the first coalition government ended. In 1998, elections were held and a government was established. 1999 was the first 12-month period they had without war, but a severe flood occurred, destroying 15% of the country. They are poorly educated and poorly skilled. Tourism was their main industry in 2002. In 2003, they held another set of elections, but it took until 2004 until the fractionated parties agreed to the election process.

Cameroon, *1961*

This country was part owned by France, part by Britain but they merged and became one in 1961. They have been trying to become a democracy but the traditional monarchy system still holds. They are a potentially wealthy African country because of oil resources but they struggle to bring their government and people into the 20th century. The also have a huge AIDS population, violence and a harsh climate in which to live. They are working at becoming a developed country.

Canada, *1867*

This country has political independence but is still tied to Great Britain, its initial founder. Its economy is similar to the U.S. (but not as wealthy) and international trade agreements in 1989 and 1994 have substantially increased their wealth. They have increasing problems between the French and English provinces, which are causing some political turmoil. This country is physically large, but much of it is uninhabitable because of permafrost and cyclonic storms that come down from the arctic. Its economy is in the trillions of dollars when it comes to industry. They also export a large amount of oil; 85% of its export is to the U.S.

Cape Verde, *1975*

This is a small island country off the coast of Africa which became independent of Portugal in 1975. They recently (1998) have been working on creating a democratic society but they have basically no natural resources except for fishing. The climate is poor, the people are poor and rely on aid to stay alive. The island is used as port for trade. They have been experiencing drought since the beginning of the 20th century.

Cayman Islands, *1863*

This Caribbean island was colonized by the British but left under Jamaican rule until 1962 when Britain took over full rule. There are no direct taxes on the island but its economy thrives on offshore banking. Over 40,000 companies use Cayman, including six large banks. A stock exchange was opened on the island in 1997 because of the large amount of banks that were using the island. 75% of its daily income is from tourism, including 600,000 U.S. tourists per year.

Central African Republic, *1993*

This recently became independent from France after years of military rule and infighting. It borders Sudan; they export timber, diamonds, coffee and cotton. Due to military fighting, the people are generally poor even though the country has resources. 70% of the population is also scattered in far reaching areas. AIDS is very high. In 1993 civilian rule was established until 2003. General Bozize overthrew the government. An election was attempted in 2005, and General Bozize was confirmed as president. The country is still in civil unrest as he does not have control of the countryside. This is one of the many countries ravaged by the diamond trade. Much of the civil war and control of the country is based on the diamond trade, which enslaves its people.

Chad, *1960*

Chad recently became independent from France, but they have been in civil war and war with Libya for three decades. This borders Sudan; they found peace in 1990 and settled disputes with Libya, then created a democratic constitution and held elections in 1996. In 1998, internal war broke out again and tentative peace was reached in 2002, but democracy has not been recognized, and the military still rules. Oil is in the land and they just started developing this with outside aid. In 2005, rebel groups from Sudan have been making probing attacks into eastern Chad to see if they can take it over. Chad's government is in the hands of the ethnic minority, and in 2005 the president removed constitutional terms of limit (meaning he can be there indefinitely).

Chile, *1810*

They had been under Marxist rule in the 70s; their first democratic rule came in 1990. The major income is trade, but the general population has a poor individual income and the government is working on increasing the standard of living. They have formed strong bonds in the international community and created a stable democratic nation.

China, *221 BC*

For centuries this was the leading civilization, but by the 20th century they had a lot of civil uprising and after WWII they became communistic and very strict. By 1978 the then leader began import/export which quadrupled the economy. Economically they function almost like a democracy but socially they are under strict military control to the degree that their daily lives have strict laws imposed on them, like how many children they can have. This has created a strong discrepancy in income, creating very wealthy and very poor people. Their land is eroding and overpopulation is a huge problem along with famine and poverty. They have a tenuous relationship with the World Trade Federation because of humanitarian reasons. Civil unrest is increasing.

Christmas Island, *1643*

This small island is in the Indian Ocean. It was named for the day of its discovery by Britain who used it for mining phosphate. The UK handed it over to Australia in 1958. Australia made two thirds of the island a national park and there are 361 people taking care of the island.

Clipperton Island, *1855*

This small isolated island west of Mexico was named after John Clipperton, a famous pirate who used it as his hideout in the early 18th century. It was annexed by France, then taken over by Mexico and eventually awarded back to France in 1855. The island is uninhabited with no ports, but the surrounding waters are used for tuna fishing.

Cocos Islands, *1609*

This is a series of 27 small islands halfway between Australia and Sri Lanka and south of Indonesia. Though discovered in 1609, they remained uninhabited until Britain took them over in 1807. Then Britain transferred them to Australia in 1955. There are two islands that are habitable and together they have a small population of 628 people. One island holds ethnic native Europeans called the West Island and on the home island, there are ethnic Malays. Coconuts are the sole cash crop. Local gardens and fishing contribute to the island food supplies but other items are brought in from Australia.

Colombia, *1830*

The country exports oil and coffee officially, but their biggest business is allegedly drug trade. Personal security and safety is the population's main problem along with declining exports. Insurgent groups are a constant problem with guerilla violence, and the government has not been able to overcome this. Neighboring countries are now seeing this spill over into their territory. The U.S. has been heavily and covertly financially involved in this country. For over 40 years, they have had to deal with antigovernment insurgent groups and paramilitary groups, both funded by the drug trade. Even the paramilitary groups and the antigovernment groups are fighting with each other for control. In 2002, paramilitary members demobilized their group for a peace process, although they continue their drug activity. At present, the government is trying to tighten control on the country and for the first time has a presence in every municipality.

Comoros, *1975*

This is an island country off of Africa that became independent of France in 1975, but has had 19 coups overtake the government since. In 1999 the military took over, and in 2002 they held their first elections. One of the poorest countries, it is made up of three islands. Fishing and forestry are their trade, but the people are poor and uneducated. Foreign aid is their main source of income. The government is struggling to upgrade education.

Congo-Brazzaville, *1960*

This separated from France in 1960 and they were a Marxist government until 1990. In 1965, this country was taken over by Joseph Mobutu. He changed his name as well as the country's, and until recently this country was known as Zaire. He stayed in power for 32 years and was a brutal dictator. The inflow of refugees from Rwanda and Burundi in 1994 led to the toppling of this regime in 1997. The country changed its name, and the Rwandan refugees along with Uganda tried to overtake the country. Troops from Angola, Chad, Namibia, Sudan and Zimbabwe intervened to support the Kinshasa regime that had been in place since 1997. A cease-fire was signed in 1999. In 2001, the president was assassinated and his son took over. In 2002, they negotiated to get the Rwandan refugees out of the Congo. Democratic since 1992, the country had its first election with a democracy in 2006. Many dictators take over a country and claim to be a democracy to get the UN off their backs and to get foreign aid money. Oil and forestry are their main exports.

Congo Republic, *1960*

This country separated from France in 1960. They were a Marxist government until 1990. They held their first democratic elections in 1992. In 1997, there was a brief war and the former Marxist president regained power. The north and south were divided and in 2003 they signed a peace accord. They have a large problem with refugees spilling over from neighboring countries at war. They were once one of Africa's largest petroleum producers, but the production is declining so they are now looking to offshore oil.

The Cook Islands, *1770*

This region is between Hawaii and New Zealand and was named after the famous pirate Captain Cook. It was under British administration until 1965 when it was transferred to New Zealand. It is self-governing in free association with New Zealand. In other words, they can be an independent country at any time, but they choose to rule themselves, while staying under the financial responsibility of New Zealand. There are approximately 21,000 people on the islands. Many of them wind up going to New Zealand and coming back. They have a lack of natural resources. Due to their location, they cannot attract any tourism but that is what they are trying to do. In the 1980s and 1990s, like many countries, it lived beyond its means and incurred a lot of debt. This has forced New Zealand to step in and help the country better their infrastructure and do more about attracting tourism.

Coral Sea Islands, *1969*

This is a set of small uninhabited islands outside of Australia that are scattered over 1 million square kilometers of the ocean in an area called the Coral Sea. It is filled with beautiful reefs and things like automated weather stations, beacons and lighthouses sitting on the islands.

Costa Rica, *1821*

This country has only had two documented periods of violence. Ironically, throughout history many countries have tried to overtake this one, but the brutal heat, mosquitoes and pirate raids were too much for them, and the invading countries left. For a short period of time, Spain did declare this as one of their dependents, but Costa Rica declared independence in 1821. Their economy is strong in agriculture and recently became involved in technology. It sits between Panama and Nicaragua and has a high standard of living with a stable democratic government with a lot of personal land ownership.

Cote d'Ivoire, *1960*

This sits in West Africa and became independent of France in 1960. They export coffee and cocoa. The country had been stable until 1999 when a military coup took control for 10 months until the current president took over. The economy had been slowly falling due to market value of cocoa beans being decreased. The president is trying to help the country diversify. AIDS is very high. In 2002 a coup was attempted, but failed. Rebel forces claimed the north half of the country. In January of 2003, they were granted ministerial positions in a unity government. Issues that sparked the civil war are unresolved and the central government has yet to exert their control over the northern regions. In 2007, violence broke out again. There are several thousand French and West African troops present trying to maintain the peace and stop civil war.

Croatia, *1991*

Prior to WWI, Croatia, along with many other territories, belonged to the then powerful Austro-Hungarian Empire. After WWI, several of the Croats, Slovenes and Serbs formed the country Yugoslavia. In 1991, Yugoslavia was dissolved and each territory became its own independent country, with all three ethnicities living in all territories. The territories remained linked by a very complex set of politics. A powerful Serb leader took the territories into a brutal four-year civil war, with much of the internal Serb population from all the territories rising up to kill within their own country. The war was extremely brutal with concentration camps, mass rapes and slaughters happening all the time. It was blatant "ethnic cleansing." Slovenia (another territory) and Croatia had been the most fiscally sound prior to the war, and after the war they were the first to recover. There are still many economic problems, including a high unemployment rate, but they are growing in strength. Their biggest problem is the same as for the other territories: the issues left behind after a brutal civil war.

Cuba, *1898*

This country has been under strict communistic rule since 1959 when Castro took over. They were being subsidized by the USSR until it fell, and have had severe financial problems since 1990. The country has had a huge problem with immigrants escaping by ocean (it's an island in the Caribbean) to get to the U.S. (about 2,800 a year). The government struggles with poverty and strong isolated military control. This country was also discovered by Christopher Columbus, and the island became prosperous back then for coffee and sugar exports. They imported some of the largest number of slaves for this work. They also became a major launching port for Spain, Mexico and Peru. Cuban independence came about from the U.S. after the Spanish-American war in 1898. After Castro took over in 1959, U.S. relations ended.

Cypress, *1960*

This is a small island off the southern coast of Turkey that separated from Britain in 1960. In 1973, Greece tried to overtake the country and Turkey helped them remain independent. The population is split between Greek Cypriots and Turkish Cypriots. In 1983, the country declared they were the "Turkish Republic of Cypress," but this is not internationally recognized. The UN is working with them to create a constitution, because until they have one, they will not be eligible for foreign aid. In 2004, the country rejected the UN brokered settlements and referendums for government. They remain a split island between the north and south. They have a serious water problem (like many islands), and tourism is their main trade.

Czech Republic, *1993*

In 1993, Czechoslovakia separated into the Czech Republic and Slovakia. Previously, it had been part of the Austro-Hungarian Empire, and then the USSR. They are a very prosperous country involved in NATO and the European Union. They separated carefully and with a stable government in place. They had already been trying to peacefully separate out of the USSR and had a lot of infrastructure in place, which allowed them to do very well within a few years of being on their own.

Denmark, *1849*

They have a strong economy, very similar to the U.S. in diversity of technology, agriculture, exports/imports. Throughout history this country has been a major power in Europe. They have a high standard of living and are very stable, yet choose not to participate in all aspects of the European Union.

Djibouti, *1977*

This borders Ethiopia and became independent of France in 1977. The country was in civil war from 1992 to 2001. Two thirds of the population live in one city, the remaining third is nomadic. They have no natural resources and live off trade from people traveling through the country (they are a port off the Red Sea and deal with import/export). They now host a U.S. military site in sub-Saharan Africa (which is a launching site into the middle east). AIDS is very high, 50% of the population is unemployed. They rely on aid for survival.

Dominica, *1978*

This Caribbean island became independent only to be dominated by a military dictator who was overthrown in 1980 by Mary Eugenia Charles, who then ran the country for 15 years. Historically, European countries (mainly France and Britain) spent a lot of years overtaking each of the Caribbean islands, and this was the last island they could take in 1763 because of the fierce resistance of the natives. They export bananas and soap. The tourism trade is slow to grow because of rocky shorelines (poor beaches) and they are attempting to set up offshore accounts. They have a 20% unemployment rate.

Dominican Republic, *1844*

Another island discovered by Christopher Columbus in 1492, it was one of the first, so it was used as a launching place to take over the other islands. This Caribbean island just off of Haiti exports coffee, sugar and tobacco, but has grown strong in tourism over the last decade. They were under a dictatorship from 1930 to 1961, which was followed by civil war until 1966. For the next 30 years, the country was back under a dictatorship, and in 1996 the international community got involved. After that, elections were held. They have a strong inequality with income, people are either poor or wealthy, and AIDS is rising.

East Timor, *1975/2002*

This country borders Indonesia and became independent of Portugal in 1975, only to be taken over by Indonesia nine days later. In the following years, about 250,000 East Timorians died fighting Indonesia. In 1999, the UN helped them begin their process of separation from Indonesia, which included sending in 8,000 troops for peace. Prior to the troops' arrival, Indonesia retaliated by commencing a large-scale "torched earth" campaign where they killed over 1,400 in a short period of time and drove over 300,000 out of the land, forcing them to become refugees. This was a very violent war. In 2002, the country was internally recognized, but by 2006 a military strike began the overt conflict again. As of today, Australia, New Zealand and Portuguese military and police are in the country. In 2007, many of their military pulled out as the UN entered. Seventy percent of the country's infrastructure has been destroyed and they just started to rebuild in 2002. They have oil just offshore for potential mining.

Ecuador, *1822*

This small country only developed a constitution in 1998 after years of conflict with Columbia, Venezuela and recently, Peru. They were one of the original Inca Empires. They export oil and bananas, but because they don't follow the World Trade Organization's standards for participation, they remain poverty-stricken despite rich resources. Their economy collapsed in 1999; they live off of loans and are rebuilding their infrastructure. By 2004, three presidents in a row had been kicked out. They are presently unstable.

Egypt, *1922*

This country sits by the Nile River and is somewhat isolated on both sides. The richness of the river and the isolation helped to create an environment where one of the world's greatest civilizations prospered in 3200 BC, which lasted over three millennia. The last Egyptian dynasty fell to Persia in 341 BC, when they were taken over by the Greeks and Romans. It was the Arabs in this country who introduced Islam to the area, and they ruled for six centuries. In 1869, Egypt became an important world transportation hub, but the country fell heavily into debt. Britain took control of their government in 1882, but in 1992 Egypt became independent again following WWII. In 1971, they built a dam on the Nile to create lakes, which greatly enriched their soil and helped ease their water problems. In the last decade, they spent tons of money to modernize their infrastructure and become more connected to the world. In the last several years, some would say they have started to go backward with their reforms though Egypt has worked hard to change with the times. Natural gases are a big exported item from this country. The country remains overly populated, gridlocked in old ways, and its people poorly educated.

El Salvador, *1821*

This is a struggling, impoverished country that keeps getting devastated by hurricanes and earthquakes and has a weak government. They are the smallest country in Central America. In 1992, they ended a 12-year civil war. In 2001, they adopted the U.S. dollar as their currency. They are trying to promote tourism and investment by strengthening their transport through their waterways. They export coffee (the U.S. is their largest buyer) and the economy is picking up. They depend heavily on outside aid, especially from the U.S.

Equatorial Guinea, *1968*

This is a series of five small islands and a small landlocked area. They became a struggling democratic society in 1998, but have yet to have the election system work. They just discovered oil, but cocoa export has been their main income. They are impoverished at this time. This country is run by a very tough dictator. The people suffer, although they have had a sudden increase in economic growth because of offshore oil discovered in the last few years. There has been no improvement in the living standard.

Eritrea, *1993*

This country spent 30 years fighting to become independent of Ethiopia. They started fighting again in 1998; in 2000, the UN was invited in, and they have agreed to leave troops to watch the border until the border dispute is worked out. They are extremely poor, sick and illiterate, and AIDS is wiping out the population fast. Agriculture is their only economy at this time.

Estonia, *1918*

It was overtaken by the USSR in 1940 and regained independence in 1991, with troops leaving in 1994. They are a strong, growing economy heavily trading with Finland and the Netherlands, and trying to connect to the U.S. It gained entrance into the EU and NATO in 2004.

Ethiopia, *unknown (over 3,000 years)*

From 1974 to 1991, a bloody military coup took place. A constitution was formed in 1994, but the country was ravaged. They are very poor, dying of AIDS and plagued by drought. Over five million people per year are fed by outside aid. They export coffee. The government owns the whole land and "leases" it to its people, which is a big problem. World organizations are present in this country trying to help its people. They remain in dispute with Eritrea regarding borders.

Europa, *1897*

This is a small uninhabited island off of Madagascar that the French took possession of in 1897. Today France has a military base on the island and it is being disputed by Madagascar.

Falkland Islands, *1690*

These islands in South America include 200 small islands and two main islands known as the East and West Falklands. They were discovered by the English, but were settled by the French in 1764. Two years later, they were turned over to Spain. For years, Britain and Spain fought over who owned the islands. Britain asserted itself by putting a naval base there in 1833. In April of 1982, Argentina invaded the islands. Britain responded with force and the conflict lasted for seven weeks before Argentina surrendered. There are about 3,000 inhabitants on the island, mainly doing fishing, with about $40 million a year farmed. The fishing revenue pays for the islands' health and education. The British are exploring oil around the island and there is evidence to suggest that there could be a lot of oil. There is an international licensing dispute between Argentina and Britain regarding who has rights to the oil.

Faroe Islands, *9ᵗʰ century*

This area includes 17 small inhabited islands in the Norwegian Sea that were originally settled by the Vikings. They have been tied to Denmark since the 14ᵗʰ century. Self-government came about in 1948, but they remain a territory of Denmark. In 1994, their economy became very strong, mostly due to fishing export. This is their only source of income, although there is believed to be oil in the sea around them.

Fiji, *1970*

This country became independent of Britain in 1970; there were two military coups in 1987 over indigenous Indians. They remained in civil unrest until 1999, when a peace agreement was reached, which lasted one year. In 2001 a democratic government was formed. It has many natural rich resources and sees a half million tourists per year. Sugar export is one third of their economy. In 2006 another military coup ousted the president, and in 2007 the general who initiated the coup appointed himself interim prime minister.

Finland, *1917*

This country has gone from forestry to industry very well and their economy is stable and they trade with the West a lot. They are a republic and have a stable government. In the 1800s they were part of Russia but gained complete independence in 1917. During WWII, this small country successfully defended itself against the Soviet Union.

France, *1789*

This is an affluent European country with close ties to the U.S. They are transitioning from an economy heavily government-owned to one that is market-owned. They are privatizing large industries like banks and airlines, which has not been done here. This creates a period of instability in their economy. They have also lowered their work week to a maximum of 35 hours; outside sources are telling them that they will have a hard time being privatized and competitive working fewer hours per week.

France is at the forefront in developing EU military capabilities and foreign policies. Over the last 10 years this country has had significant riot issues with immigrants living in France who claim that the government promotes prejudice against outsiders because they are unable to get work due to their ethnicity. The government did not deny it, but now claims it is working to change the internal system.

French Guiana, *1604*

This sits in South America next to Brazil off the coast of North America. The French used this as a prison until 1951. It was notorious as a harsh prison. Today the European Space Agency launches its satellites from here. Its other income is fishing and forestry. Ninety percent of the country is covered in woodlands.

French Polynesia, *1946*

This is a series of small islands between South America and Australia, four of which are volcanic rocks. The French annexed these Polynesian islands. In 1995, France used the island of Mururoa for nuclear testing. After widespread protest, the tests were stopped in 1996. There are 270,000 people living here and French military bases. They also do pearl farming and deep sea fishing.

French Southern and Antarctic Lands, *1840*

This lies south of Africa and the Indian Ocean. There have been as many as 145 researchers living here at one time to research things like global warming. The U.S. does not recognize France's right to own the southern half of the Antarctic Ocean.

Gabon, *1960*

Since becoming independent from France, they have had autocratic rule until 1991, when they developed a democratic constitution and received political/economic guidance from international sources. They have done very well for a country in Africa. They have a very high AIDS rate. Exporting oil is their income source, but they struggle with being "young" by overspending and failing to pay loans back, which causes withdrawal of support. President Bongo is a dictator and elections from 2002 to 2005 have exposed the corruptness and weakness of the government. Despite this, a small population and abundant natural resources and foreign aid have kept Gabon prosperous.

Gambia, *1965*

This African country was engaged in border wars from 1982 to 1989, and then in internal war in 1994. In 1996, they developed a constitution and held elections then and in 2000. Unemployment is very high, they have no natural resources except for peanuts, but trade has diminished. They are struggling to educate and create an economy. Jammeh led the military coup in 1994 and has been elected president since.

Gaza Strip, *1993*

This is a highly disputed piece of land in the Middle East. The dispute is over religion. The land itself has no natural resources, has severe water problems and the country has no stable economy. This piece of land has been fought over for thousands of years and has a very complex history. The Gaza Strip and the West Bank are areas, like cities, within Israel. Palestine claims that these areas within Israel are theirs. After WWII, like many major wars, land borders were redefined all over Europe and the Middle East. The people who made up Israel waited a long time to claim this land and they did so after WWII. Before the war, the land belonged to Palestine. This is the heart of the dispute. They both want it for religious reasons. Neighboring countries Syria and Libya are also involved in this dispute. Many agreements have been signed and broken on both sides. Despite this, both Israel and Palestine still have disputes over the Gaza Strip. In 2005, Israel agreed to withdraw from the Gaza Strip. But Israel still controls the ports, the air space and most access roads to the Gaza Strip. In 2006, a new government was elected in Palestine, led by Hamas, a group that refuses to acknowledge Israel. The countries continue to fight for this land.

Germany, *1871*

After trying to take over Europe twice, this country struggled with political, economic and social reform as well as living with their neighbors and their brutal history under Hitler. Under his rule this country caused terror throughout the world while systematically torturing and killing millions of people. Following WWII, they split off into two countries, but reunited in 1990. Since then, their economy has become one of the strongest in Europe and helped to create the European Union. The country that tried to overtake Europe is now trying to help grow all the countries financially by bringing them up to higher standards. Their biggest financial problem is absorbing former East Germany's $70 million debt. Their population has become elderly with a huge gap in the average adult age due to the war years. They also have a hush-hush problem internally with the young generation forming white supremacy/Hitler-like gangs. In 2006, Angela Merkel took over as chancellor in a very contested election. Among other things, she is from the old eastern half of the country which was under communistic rule until 1990. In 2007 she was called "the most powerful woman in the world" by Forbes magazine.

Georgia, 1991

This became independent of Russia in 1991. They have a goal of becoming democratic, but the Russian military is still there and they have infighting going on. Their economy is based on agriculture, especially nuts and citrus. They are struggling in their new economy and trying to privatize. They are counting on future trades to increase economy. In 2003, the incumbent government tried to manipulate elections that set off large protests. In 2004, the government changed hands, but they still have two civil conflicts in outlying regions. Abkhazia and South Ossetia are the two outlying regions that the central government does not have control over, and they are supported by Russia. Russia peace-keeping operations are helping this country to unite.

Ghana, 1957

Two countries seceded from Britain to form this country in Africa. They had a lot of coups until 1981, when they formed a constitution, and then formed another in 1991. They have lots of natural resources like gold, timber and cocoa, but rely on foreign aid because of poor education and poor economy to be able to maximize their resources. They are heavily in debt and under a relief program.

Gibraltar, 1830

This is actually the southernmost tip of Spain. In a treaty in 1713, it was given over to Britain and was formally declared a colony in 1830. In 1960 and 2002, Spain pressured Gibraltar to become independent of Britain, and they refused. They voted to stay a part of British dependency. They are self-sufficient with a large shipping trade, offshore banking and an international conference center. There is a British military presence here.

Glorioso Islands, *1892*

This includes two highly vegetated coral islands and three rock islands in the Indian Ocean. France holds it as a military launching place. There are no indigenous inhabitants beyond the French military and a few scientists.

Greece, *1829*

This country was part of the Ottoman Empire in the 1800s. After that empire fell, they acquired several islands (by the 20th century). During WWII they were invaded by Italy, and then Germany. They internally fought off communist rebels until 1949. Greece joined NATO in 1959, but from 1967 to 1974, they had a military dictatorship, which put their government on hold and ousted the then-ruling king. When this period ended, they formed their own democracy and ended monarchy rule. They have a moderate economy; a lot of it based on tourism. They are trying to privatize business, reduce taxes and overhaul their economy.

Greenland, *1978*

This country separated from Denmark in 1988. They are an island that has 81% of its landmass covered in ice caps. It's actually the world's largest island. Denmark still deals with their foreign affairs. Their economy is based on exporting fish and support from Denmark.

Grenada, *1974*

This small Caribbean island was settled by the French in the 17th century. Later, Britain would take control and use slaves to expand the sugar crop industry. Production of cacao (for chocolate), and eventually nutmeg surpassed the sugar industry. In 1967, Britain gave autonomy to the country, and eventually it became independent. A decade later, it was invaded by Marxist military (from Cuba) in 1983. The U.S. military went in six days later to stop the takeover. Democratic elections were held by 1984. Tourism is their main source of income today, which has been declining, and their national debt is on the rise. They have also been hit seriously by hurricanes and are trying to develop offshore accounts.

Guadeloupe, *1635*

This Caribbean island is part of St. Martin. St. Martin is shared with the Netherlands. The southern part is owned by the Netherlands and is called

Sint Maarten. The northern part is Guadeloupe, but commonly called St. Martin.

Guam, *1898*

This small island sits between Hawaii and the Philippines. Spain ceded this country to the U.S. The U.S. lost it to Japan, and then got it back after WWII. This island has the most strategically important military bases in the Pacific for the U.S.

Guatemala, *1821*

There was a 36-year guerilla war which ended in 1996 after killing off over 100,000 people. This former Mayan region experienced three centuries of Spanish rule before gaining its independence. Two thirds of their income is exported coffee, sugar and bananas, and they recently signed a treaty with Mexico for exporting their goods. The current president is new and is looking to revise the privatization policy which creates uncertainty at this time for economic futures.

Guernsey and Jersey Islands, *1945*

This small set of islands sits in the English Channel. In medieval times, it held the Dukedom of Normandy, which held sway over both France and England for a time. During WWII, this was the only British soil occupied by German troops. Today, 55% of its income is financial services and insurance. Its income used to be based on tomatoes and cut flowers. It has a very low taxation rate, making it favorable to banks.

Guinea, *1958*

This is a small country in West Africa that has had democratic rule since the 80s, but only two Presidents elected. Their biggest problem right now is that civil war in the countries next to them (Sierra Leone and Liberia) has spilled over onto their land. This country remains underdeveloped, even though they have good resources of minerals and hydropower. 75% of their income is from exporting their goods, but their money is used to protect two different borders. The people are very uneducated and unskilled. In 2006 the country's economy was slipping, two major strikes happened in their work force and there continues to be social unrest.

Guinea-Bissau, *1974*

They had their first free elections in 1994, but then had a bloody uprising in 1998 that was not over until 2001. Its economy was wiped out in war and they are just starting to create another democracy. This makes it one of the top 10 poorest countries in the world. Rice was their major crop. They are starving, with no real economy and living on aid, but they do have unexplored offshore oil. The newly elected president was also the general who headed a coup in 1980 that plunged the country into unrest. He spent years ignoring government while "cleansing" the country of anyone who would oppose him. Despite that, the country has elected him twice. From 2001 to 2003, a democratic president was in office but was ousted by Vieira who was again formally elected in 2005.

Guyana, *1966*

In 1989, Guyana launched a "recovery program," which took the country out of an impoverished socialistic state to democratic free trade. This is formally a British controlled area that in the 17th and 18th centuries was one of the major areas where slaves were sold. Mining and sugar is their industry. They struggle with a poor work force, external debt and AIDS, but they are doing well considering how impoverished they were when they started.

Haiti, *1804*

The French took over this island in 17th century and France and Spain fought over the island for many years. Then they imported a huge amount of slaves, one of the largest imports of slaves. Then a half a million of the slaves revolted, taking over the island and giving it its independence in 1804, becoming the very first black republic. They experienced three decades of dictatorship which ended in 1990 with free elections, but then a military coup took place. They have been involved in internal war since their inception and are one of the poorest countries. Over 80% of the population live in abject poverty, dying of starvation. In 2000, the U.S. and the EU suspended all help going to Haiti, telling them that aid would only return when they stopped fighting. In 2004, the interim president cut a deal with the UN and allowed a stabilization mission to come in so they could receive aid. In 2006, they elected a democratic president and created a parliament.

Heard and McDonald Islands, *1947*

This is a set of uninhabited Antarctic islands that are populated by a large number of seals. The land has been designated a nature preserve. It is 80% covered in ice.

Holy See (Vatican City), *1929*

This piece of land resides within the boundaries of Italy inside the city of Rome. For more than a thousand years, popes ruled portions of the Italian peninsula. In the mid-19th century, many of the areas that popes ruled were seized by newly formed countries, including the kingdom of Italy. In 1870, the popes' holdings were further limited as Rome itself was annexed into a city. In 1929, disputes between the popes and Italy were resolved with a series of treaties, which basically established Vatican City. In these agreements, Roman Catholicism was given a special status, basically making all Catholics in Italy part of this "country." In 1984, this was modified, including the part where Roman Catholics were seen as part of this independent state. There are formally 920 people living in the Holy See. Economically, its income comes from Catholics all over the world. They get to remain separate from Italy's taxation. This "country" does not have formal status at the UN.

Honduras, *1821*

After two decades of infighting they formed an independent government in 1982. They are very poor, uneducated and rely on aid for survival. They have severe escalating crime and gangs. Their government is unstable at this time. This country became a haven for neighboring El Salvador's guerrillas. They have also sustained billions of dollars' worth of hurricane damage.

Hong Kong, *1841*

This country originally belonged to China, but was ceded to Britain in 1841. In the 19th century, the boundaries of Hong Kong were more formally delineated. Britain's occupation from its original agreement with China had a time limit on it, and in 1984 it went back to China and became the Hong Kong Special Administrative Region. China agreed, after much debate, because at this time China had a very poor humanitarian rating with the UN, to maintain a "one country, two systems" formula. They agreed not to impose their socialist system on Hong Kong for 50 years, but they control 100% of military defense affairs. This was a very serious event at the time, as Hong Kong was one of the largest cities in the world, very international, very prosperous and very western. At the time, China was opposed to all of this. Chinese was not formally imposed until July of 1997.

Howland Island, *1857*

It is a small island halfway between Hawaii and Australia. For about 40 years, in the 1800s, the U.S. and Britain mined this island. Today it is a national wildlife refuge.

Hungary, *1991*

Became independent after the USSR fell, but they had been fighting for it since 1956. They were the country that broke the Warsaw Pact, but went through years of war with Russia. They have strong relations with the U.S. and NATO. They are working on healthcare reform and tax reform.

Iceland, *903/1944*

This country had the world's oldest legislative assembly called the Althing. It was independent for 300 years before being overtaken by Norway and Denmark because of volcanic eruption in 1875 that devastated their economy and caused widespread famine. Twenty percent of the population immigrated to Canada after this disaster. They became independent from Denmark in 1944. They have a strong economy and one of the highest standards of living in the world. They have an extensive welfare system with very little unemployment. They are opposed to joining the EU because they don't want their fishing export regulated.

India, *over 5000 years*

From the 8th to the 19th century, India experienced a lot of Arab and European invasions. Gandhi, a famous activist, led this country to independence from Britain in 1947, but was later killed as a result of internal conflict. The continent was then divided into India and Pakistan. Another war between these countries in 1971 led to East Pakistan becoming the country of Bangladesh. They are extremely overpopulated, impoverished and have constant civil unrest based on ethnic and religious differences. Their economy is based on local agriculture, but over the last eight years western industry has taken a strong hold in this country, bringing financial independence to its young people for the very first time. This is challenging the old cultural ways, bringing in new ideas and change for the country. One quarter of the population is starving to death. There is a percentage of the population educated well in English, and they have a strong software exporting business. Aid is common in this country and so is internal violence over ethnicity. AIDS has grown fast. They also have an ongoing dispute with Pakistan over an area called Kashmir. Both Pakistan and India have nuclear capability. They are also routinely hit by floods in the fall. In the late 90s, 20,000 people died from flooding in one day.

Indian Ocean

This body of water sits between Africa, Australia and Asia. It is the major sea route connecting the Middle East, Africa and Asia with the Americas and Europe. Its heaviest traffic is petroleum and oil products. Forty percent of oil production comes through this body of water. The surrounding countries, like Africa, Indonesia and Thailand, have beaches with sand that are rich in minerals.

Indonesia, *1949*

They had a severe internal conflict which ended up separating out a piece of the land which became its own county, East Timor, in 1999. To this day, Indonesia is still attacking East Timor, and UN peace keepers along with Australian military sit in East Timor to deal with the violence and try and keep peace. This was the country decimated by the 2004 tsunami, which was followed by an earthquake a few months later. Because of their internal strife and anger at outside interference, they refused much of the help offered after these devastating events. This is the world's largest set of small islands grouped together. It is also the home to the world's largest Muslim population and believed to be heavily involved in al-Qaeda. They are struggling to become an election-based government. They would like to advance internationally, but resist conforming to international law. They have a severely depressed economy, a corrupt government, unstable banking and war at their borders, which they cannot defend. In 2002, they agreed to reform in order to receive IMF aid but have yet to do so.

Iran, *1935*

Prior to 1935, they were known as Persia and have been around longer than any recorded history. In 1979 they became a military Islamic republic, meaning that their government is based on both their religion and military control. It was also in this year that U.S. relations became tense because the U.S. embassy in Tehran, Iran was seized by students. From 1980 to 1988, they fought a bloody war with Iraq over land that was never resolved and supposedly became (unofficially) associated with the U.S. by trading oil for arms weapons. But at this time, the war between Iran and Iraq spilled out into the gulf and there were some military conflicts between Iran and the U.S. Navy, so the relationship was complex and unstable. Also, in the 1980s Iran had conflicts with Lebanon and some other countries, with the U.S. responding by sanctioning Iran and forming stronger ties with Saudi Arabia. In the 1990s and early 2000s, Iran had some governmental changes to a more conservative base and attempted to make some connections on the international level. At present they are considered a "danger" by the U.S. government because of their overt criticism of the war the U.S. is in with Iraq as well as the international community trying to impose sanctions on them regarding their nuclear program. The UN and U.S. are opposed to Iran having nuclear capability, and Iran states that they have just as much right as any other industrialized country to have this energy. They have not diversified outside of oil and their economy has been diminishing. They also have a large discrepancy between the wealthy and the poor.

Iraq, 1932

Initially this was part of the Ottoman Empire and Britain took occupation during WWI. In a series of stages, Iraq attained its independence in 1932. In 1958, it claimed that it was now a republic, but in truth it had just gone through a series of dictators. The last one was Saddam Hussein. They had a war with their neighbor Iran from 1980 to 1988 over territory. In 1990, Iraq seized Kuwait, which is a very small country at the tip of Iraq that has strong ties to the U.S. because of oil. U.S.-led forces went in to expel Iraq out of Kuwait in 1991 and it was called the Gulf War. Following this, the UN security counsel required Iraq to get rid of all of its weapons of mass destruction and long-range missiles. Iraq was non-compliant for 12 years. The U.S. led international forces into Iraq in 2003 and ousted Saddam Hussein and his regime. At present, the U.S. remains in Iraq which has fallen into civil war. The U.S. is in internal conflict as to what to do about this country's stability. Internationally, the U.S. rationalized its invasion by claiming that Iraq was a danger to the world. Once inside the country, it was found that the people were starving, there was a very poor infrastructure, a weak army and no weapons of mass destruction. The U.S. invaded against UN mandates and under heavy protest from countries all over the world.

Ireland, *1921*

This island, next to Britain, was inhabited by Celtic tribes from 600 to 150 BC. Then the Norsemen took over. Britain then invaded and fought on this land for seven centuries. In 1916, there was a particularly violent Easter that began several years of hard-core guerrilla warfare that ended in Ireland becoming its own country in 1921. Twenty-six southern counties became independent, while six northern counties remained part of Britain. In 1948, the southern counties withdrew from the British Commonwealth and joined the European Community (later to become the EU) in 1973. There has been chronic infighting through a group called the IRA since the country became separated. They are considered terrorists and fight against British rule. A peace agreement between south and north was signed in 1998 (not recognized by the IRA) and is being implemented. By 2006 the IRA agreed to recognize the Good Friday Agreement drafted in 1998. Their economy is based on trade; formerly it was based on agriculture and the country had been very impoverished. Though the economy has improved, violence and infighting is still a large problem. There is a huge economic difference between Britain-controlled Ireland and independent Ireland, which is part of the real reason behind the fighting more so than religion, which is often what the news promotes.

Isle of Man, *1765*

This is an island between Great Britain and Ireland that was held by the Norwegians in the 13th century. Then it went to Scotland, until finally coming under British rule. There are about 75,000 people living on the island and their major income is offshore banking with some tourism.

Israel, *1948*

This country used to be Palestine. After WWII, Britain withdrew from Palestine and the country was divided into two communities: Arab (Palestine) and Jewish (Israel). The people rejected living together. Initially the Jewish people separated out land they named Israel. The U.S., along with the UN was influential in Israel being formed. The Israeli borders have been in constant dispute since its inception; wars in 1967, 1979, 1982, 1991, 1994, 1998 and 2000 were all about borders. They are agriculturally self-sufficient, and they export diamonds and high-tech equipment. They have no natural oil resources. The land is considered "holy" by Muslims, Jews and Christians. Their biggest dispute is with an area called the Gaza Strip, which borders the Mediterranean Sea, and the West Bank, which borders Jordan. Basically, Palestinians consider these areas "Palestine," though they are under Israeli rule. Technically, both areas are trying to become an independent country: WBGS (the West Bank and Gaza Strip). After years of violence, bitterness is a constant problem. In 2000, Israel agreed to withdraw from Lebanon, which it had occupied. The borders are still in dispute and violence increased from 2003 to 2005. In 2005, the U.S. was part of an international team that went in to help create (another) peace agreement, but in 2006 the terrorist group Hamas was elected into government in Palestine setting off a huge wave of issues, including freezing agreements between Israel and Palestine. Lebanon, which is a border country and home to Hamas, was involved with a 34-day violent conflict with Israel in 2006. Israel was in the process of withdrawing from Gaza, but the newly elected prime minister stopped this process due to Hamas rule. They are fighting today.

Italy, *1861*

In 1920, Mussolini created a fascist government and aligned himself with Hitler in WWII. After the war, a democratic republic was formed. The north is prosperous but the south remains more financially challenged. They supposedly have a large problem with organized crime. Tourism is their big revenue. They have high unemployment and low income. They have a large welfare system. They often home-school their kids, and kids usually stay at home until they're married, even if it's in their thirties or forties.

Jamaica, *1962*

This Caribbean island was discovered by Columbus and settled by the Spanish, who exterminated the native Indian population and then populated it with slaves from Africa. Britain took the island in 1655 and took over the plantation economy. Most of the Caribbean islands banded together after WWII, and in 1958 they formed the Federation of the West Indies, where eventually they became independent. This island separated from Britain in 1962. Severe economic depression hit in the 70s, which led to internal fighting and decreased tourism. The country split into two serious gangs who controlled the government and created a strong drug trafficking economy. In 1980, and again in 1990, the entire government changed. Civil violence and unrest is increasing, along with a strong division between the wealthy and the poor. Their economy is heavily dependent on U.S. tourism, which has dramatically decreased since 9/11.

Jan Mayen Island, 1614

This uninhabited island sits between Greenland and Norway. Occasionally, it is used by seal hunters and there is a large volcano on the island that became active in 1970. It is the northern-most active volcano on Earth.

Japan, 1962

After a large defeat in WWII, this country has adopted Western economic culture while keeping their social culture. They are second only to the U.S. as the largest economy. Though they have an emperor, the country is really run by the government body. The economy dramatically decreased in the 90s after too much increase in the 80s. Robotics is one of their largest exports (there are about 700,000 robotics used on the planet; 400,000 are made here). The country now deals with overcrowding, an aging population and a younger generation not as obsessively focused as the previous generation.

Jarvis Island, 1821

This island sits in the South Pacific and was mined in the U.S. until 1879. Britain took over the island for a while but never did anything with it. The U.S. reclaimed it in 1935, and today it is a national wildlife refuge.

Johnston Atoll, 1855

This small island sits right off of Honolulu, Hawaii, and was mined by the U.S. until 1880. It was taken over by the U.S. Navy in 1934, and then the U.S. Air Force in 1938. In the 1950s and 60s it was used for nuclear tests, and until the year 2000 it was used for storage and as a disposal site for chemical weapons. In 2005, the facilities were all closed.

Jordan, *1946*

After becoming independent from Britain, this country was ruled by King Hussein from 1956 to 1999. He was a strong ruler who kept the country intact; the country was being sought after by the U.S., USSR, UK, several Arab nations, Israel and internal Palestinian forces. Several coups were attempted unsuccessfully. In 1989, parliament elections started and he began liberating the country. In 1994, he signed a peace agreement with Israel. He died in 1999 and his son took over formal power. They don't have much oil, water is needed and the people are impoverished and poorly educated. The new leader is putting the country under reform, developing trade agreements with the U.S. and WTO and trying to modernize his country. The king's wife is often considered an asset as she follows tradition while promoting western growth, and she has lectured on the international circuit.

Juan de Nova Island, *1897*

This small island sits in the Mozambique Channel off of South Africa and was named after a famous Spanish explorer. It was exploited for its mineral deposits, and today there is a small French military base and meteorological station.

Kazakhstan, *1991*

This country became independent of the USSR and sits between Russia and China. The people were traditionally nomadic and are a mix of Turks, Mongolians and Russians. Their biggest problems include unifying the people, forming an identity and a strong economy. They have a lot of natural resources to be developed. Between 1995 and 1997, they privatized business and opened a pipeline. Their economy is growing, but they have internal strife. They are known for having a harsh government and many humanitarian issues. In recent years, there's been an issue with neighboring Uzbekistan's refugees spilling over. These refugees are cared for by the UN in tents at the border, but still the Kazakhstan government fights the situation.

Kenya, *1963*

In 1963 local icon President Kenyatta led Kenya to independence and kept the country stable until his death in 1978. In 1982, the ruling party called the Kenya African National Union (KANU) took control of the legal system, and the country fractured into the multiple ethnicities that made it up. In 1991, there were many internal groups and multiple cultures trying to function independently, and the government was forced to allow liberation to the individual different fractions within the country. From 1992 to 1997, the fractured culture failed to oust KANU, and the current president has held the country together, but per their constitution, he had to step down at the 2003 election. KANU lost this election, but then the new government fractured in 2005. Kenya used to be the largest area of trade in Africa, but due to violence this has decreased. The population has potentially the highest rate of AIDS infection in the world. They have been in severe drought for several years, and the people die in large numbers every year from war and disease. The government is corrupt and the country relies heavily on outside aid. The IMF pulled out in 2000 because the government did not maintain promised reforms.

Kingman Reef, 1922

This is a small island off of Hawaii that is today a U.S. national wildlife refuge. In the 1930s, it had a station for flying boats that were traveling from Hawaii to American Samoa. It is uninhabited.

Kiribati, 1979

This used to be a series of islands call Gilbert, Phoenix and Line (sitting between Fiji and Hawaii). Both the U.S. and the UK owned certain islands. They became independent of the UK in 1971, and of the U.S. in 1979. There are actually 33 islands/coral atolls. The economy is fishing and tourism, but the land is not very livable and the people untrained in much outside of fishing. They receive a lot of foreign aid.

Kuwait, 1961

This small country holds 10% of the world's present refined oil. From 1899 to 1961, Britain oversaw this country. It sits on the border of Iraq and was taken over by them in 1990. The U.S. and UN went to war for Kuwait in 1991 and won its liberation in four days. War continued around the area for two years. The country claims it has cost them five billion dollars to rebuild their infrastructure. The al-Sabah family has ruled throughout its history. Due to poor soil, they rely almost completely on sources outside of themselves for food.

Kyrgyzstan, *1991*

This country sits outside of China, and had been annexed into the USSR back in 1864. It is a beautiful but poor mountainous state. In 2005, they changed over to a more democratic type of private industry. It exports gold, minerals and electricity to surrounding countries. They have a serious issue with poverty, but in 2001 they started working with international organizations to help them change. They also have a supposed problem with terrorists living and working out of their country.

Laos, *1949*

This sits between Vietnam and Thailand and used to be incorporated into both, then it was under the control of Siam (later to become Thailand), and then France took over and made it part of Indochina. In 1907, the borders of Thailand and Laos were defined as they are today, and then in 1979 a communist ruler named Pathet Lao took over the country (renaming it) and ended six centuries of a ruling monarchy. Initially they only had relations with Vietnam, but by 1986 they started to decentralize and privatize. They are one of the few remaining official Communist states and still remain primitive with very little telephone systems, no transport system (including trains) and electricity in only a few areas. They are now getting aid from IMF and assistance in growth through international organizations.

Latvia, *1991*

This country separated out from Russia, but 30% of the population is still Russian, which is a concern for the Russian government. Trade is their commerce and they gradually pulled away from Russia and started trading with other countries, building their economy until they could join the WTO in 1998. They still have a very high deficit, but joined NATO and the EU.

Lebanon, *1943*

Back in the early 1900s, this country had been part of Syria (ruled by the Ottoman Empire) and was taken over by France. France separated out a part of the country, Lebanon, and gave it independence in 1943. This country ended a 15-year civil war (1976-1991) with a devastated infrastructure. The war was between Muslims and non-Muslims and ended when the Arab community stepped in to form a treaty and sent in about 16,000 Syrian troops. Syria did not remove its troops until 2005 after a very long diplomatic process. Syria, among other Middle Eastern countries, did not believe that the Muslim community was being given enough fairness in Lebanon. There was a time in which Israel also invaded southern Lebanon, claiming they were doing it for "peace reasons." In 2005, a former prime minister along with 20 others were assassinated which led to massive fighting and demonstrations. In the south of Lebanon, one particular group called Hezbollah remains strong. During the 15-year internal war, several hard-core guerrilla groups were formed, and Hezbollah is one that remains and basically controls southern Lebanon. In 2006, Hezbollah openly engaged in conflict with neighboring Israel. Hezbollah is considered a terrorist group among some in the international community. This country used to be the Arab banking hub but that economy was destroyed during the 15-year war. The country is impoverished now and trying to rebuild, but peace is not stable at this time. The Christians, though the minority, hold power in this country in the north. Some say Hezbollah unofficially runs the south. This country has been accused of housing terrorists. It is in this area of the Middle East that the Israelis (Jewish), Christians and Muslims have fought some bloody battles in the last 20 years.

Lesotho, 1966

This African country, previously held by Britain, was under 23 years of brutal military rule until 1990 when the ruler was exiled. In 1992 he returned and by 1995 was back in power. A constitutional government was started in 1993, but elections were questionable. In 1998 a violent uprising followed the elections; it was short but very violent and was stopped by outside African and neighboring Botswana military forces. In 2002 a new constitution was formed. One quarter of the population died of AIDS by 2001. Their economy is growing in apparel manufacturing. They developed a hydropower plant in 1998 and now sell water to other African countries. They are involved with a poverty reduction plan with the IMF.

Liberia, 1847

This country was created between 1822 and 1847 by the U.S. as a settlement for freed slaves. In 1847 they called themselves the Americo-Liberians and established a formal republic. From 1944 to 1971, the then president created strong foreign investments to increase the economic and social gaps that this country had between the indigenous people living there and the settlers from America. In 1980, a military coup took the country into a decade of authoritarian rule. In 1989, Charles Taylor, unofficially backed by the U.S., started a coup that developed into a very bloody civil war where the previous government and followers were systematically killed. In 1997, there was a short period of peace, and Taylor was officially elected. By 2000 fighting had resumed. The U.S. tried diplomacy to oust the very person they armed and put into office, but it didn't work and by 2003 Taylor was forcibly exiled to Nigeria. Two years of fighting followed, and the UN stepped in with armed forces. They are still there, disarming soldiers, but the country is still volatile. Taylor attempted to come back, but was killed. Their infrastructure is poor, especially because the businessmen (internal and external) fled during the war. They mine diamonds and timber, but in 2001 the UN imposed sanctions on this and banned travel outside the country because of Liberia's support to rebel factions in Sierra Leone.

Libya, *1911*

The Italians took this land from the Ottoman Turks in 1911, but lost it in WWII. After that the UN took hold of the country until it could achieve its own independence in 1951. The present ruler took over the country forcibly in 1969 and created his own government called the "Third International Theory," which is a combination of socialism and Islamic beliefs. In the 70s and 80s he supposedly used money from the country's sale of oil to spread his philosophy in other Arab nations, and supported terrorism. He pulled his troops out of Chad in 1987 (the last country he tried to take over), and the UN sanctioned the whole country in 1992 after they blew up Pan Am Flight 103. In 1999, the sanctions were withdrawn after Libya took responsibility for and made payments toward the families of Flight 103, several bombings they committed in Europe, including the downing of another plane (a French airliner). They started creating international relations and worked with the UN, stopping its nuclear program and terrorist camps. In 2006, the U.S. formally resumed diplomatic relations with Libya and rescinded its listing of Libya as a terrorist state.

Liechtenstein, *1719*

This country sits between Austria and Switzerland and is small with minimal natural resources. They are aligned with Switzerland and their banking industry was doing very well until the late 90s when lots of regulatory banking issues came up followed by the discovery of money laundering in large financial institutes. By 2003, they had developed anti-laundering laws in the country and developed a treaty with the U.S. around the legalities of international banking. They have a strong economy, a high standard of living and follow Swiss laws and customs. They have to import 90% of their goods.

Lithuania, *1990*

This was the first Soviet district to separate out and become its own independent country. They traded mainly with Russia, but Russia's economy crashed in 1998, and so did theirs. They are now looking to trade with the West, are in the WTO, NATO and the EU after privatizing business. Today their economy is doing very well.

Luxembourg, *1963*

This country was once part of the Netherlands, but lost half its land in the 1800s to Belgium in order to gain a larger state of autonomy from the Netherlands. It claimed neutrality in Europe, but after being taken over in both world wars it joined with NATO and other international organizations. It was one of the founding countries for the European Community (which became the EU). The economy is very stable and they have high industry.

Macau, *1987*

This is a small area on the southern tip of China that was colonized by Portugal in the 16th century. It was the first European settlement in the Far East. China and Portugal came to an agreement in 1987, giving the land back to China. The country has 50 years before it will be taken over completely by China's socialistic government.

Macedonia, *1991*

This country became independent of Yugoslavia in 1991 after a bloody civil war. This was the least developed principality of Yugoslavia. In 1996, they had a long dispute with Greece over the color of their flag, which hindered trade agreements; this did not end until 2004. In 2001, an insurgency broke out with ethnic Albanians living in the country. The UN and European community got involved to broker a treaty. Their infrastructure is very weak, but with help from the international community they are trying to build an economy. Their internal issues are still a high risk, and neighboring Kosovo's instability is adding to their social instability.

Madagascar, *1960*

Formerly a colony of France, this country had a 17-year dictatorship that ended in 1993 with their first free elections. Elections after that have been disputed and filled with claims of illegal activity. Agriculture has been their economy but the land is used up. They are in poverty, malnourished and have problems with healthcare and education. The land used to be rich with forest, but it was cut down to provide heat. The country has been in involved with constant demonstrations and infighting since the first elections and the 2001 elections brought violence. They are unstable.

Malawi, *1964*

This African country held its first elections in 1994 after 17 years of autocratic rule. This is one of the least developed countries with 90% of the population living off the land in rural areas. The government is new and has to develop an economy from the ground up. They are fighting corruption, AIDS, population growth and healing abuses from the previous regime. They get help from International Relief and the World Bank.

Malaysia, *1957*

This is a set of islands that was originally colonized by Britain and then occupied by Japan before becoming independent. They are split up into two islands, one connected to Thailand, the other to Indonesia. Their economy really grew from 1971 to 1990 because of exports, then a new government took over and diversified into textiles and tourism. Their textile industry is filled with forced labor. Their economy is very dependent on the U.S. and Japan.

Maldives, *1965*

This is a series of islands south of India, formerly ruled by the Dutch and then the British, whose economy is tourism and fishing. In 2004 there were riots, forcing the autocratic government to change to a more people-represented government. Eighty percent of the island land is only one meter above sea level. They are very concerned about global warming because they have seen its effects increase as their land mass decreases.

Mali, *1960*

This sits next to Algeria and was under sultan dictatorship until 1991 when a coup brought about the first democratic elections, held in 1992. Prior to that, it had been part of Senegal. Sixty-five percent of the land is pure desert; they are one of the poorest countries in the world. They are heavily dependent on foreign aid and work hard on ending corruption in the country. Ten percent of the culture remains nomadic, the rest is learning industry.

Malta, *1964*

After separating from Britain this small island spent the last 15 years building up tourism and freight shipment. It has a great location in the Mediterranean Sea and joined the EU in 2004.

Marshall Islands, *1986*

This recently became independent of the U.S. This is a series of small islands and reefs between Hawaii and Australia. The U.S. gives about $39 million a year to this struggling country that exports coconuts and other fruits. They are also making reparations for using this and other neighboring islands for nuclear testing. They have few natural resources and are trying to build tourism.

Mauritania, *1960*

This is near Algeria and after years of fighting, they separated the land (the southern half became South Sahara) and developed their own constitution in 1991. Elections have been corrupt, and today they still remain a one-party state. In 2005, a coup over took the government and put it under military rule, who claimed they would keep power for two years until uncorrupted elections could be held. In 2006 and 2007 elections were held, but at present the country is still under military autocratic rule until the president assumes power. Their population is black and native Arabs; they have tense ethnic relationships. They have had drought for 20 years forcing the nomads (half of the populace) to live in the city and find work. They export iron ore. They potentially have oil offshore but this has not been fully explored. They are impoverished.

Mauritius, *1968*

This is a small island off Madagascar (Africa) held by many nations. It became independent of Britain in 1968 and formed a democracy. It is one of the highest income countries in Africa exporting sugar. It has a high standard of human rights (for the area) which attracted investors, helping to create a very stable government. Over the last few years, weather issues and declining sugar sales have decreased income, causing some unrest in the Creole community.

Mexico, *1810*

In 1994 their economy took a huge dip creating a severe depression, but has been recovering well. They have problems with unemployment, unequal wages, overpopulation and education. They also have a huge problem with their citizens illegally crossing over into U.S. territory, creating tension between the two governments. In 2000, the ruling party was overthrown in an election. This was the first time since the 1910 Mexican Revolution that the opposition defeated the ruling party. Their industry is both modern and very outdated. The southern regions are an Indian culture and very poor with corrupt business and government as well as drug trafficking. Trade has tripled with the U.S., but there are concerns about wages and workers' environment in Mexico, especially with U.S. companies that are right over the border and running unsafe practices with very poor wages. This is a rich country that has the wealth held within a very small percentage of the people. The majority of Mexicans are very poor. They have also been hit by three devastating earthquakes in the last 10 years, one right in the heart of Mexico City. Tourism, especially from America, is very high.

Mayetta, *1843*

This is one of a series of small islands off of Southern Africa. It is the only island that voted to maintain its connection with France and forgo its independence. Their economy is based on fishing and personal farming. They are not self-sufficient and the majority of their foods and goods come from France. It is too remote for tourism.

Micronesia, *1986*

This is a series of small islands to the north of the Indonesian islands owned by the U.S. until 1986. In 1971, the U.S. helped the country start its own constitution preparing for independence. Their economy is based on fishing but they have overused the water and they remain too dependent on the U.S. to provide their income. Between 1986 and 2001 they received $1.3 billion of assistance from the U.S. Their struggle now is to do it on their own.

Midway Island, *1867*

These two small islands sit between Honolulu and Tokyo. They are uninhabited and mostly volcanic rock. The U.S. uses them for laying transpacific cable. During WWII they were used as a refueling base for the U.S. Navy. Today they are a national wildlife refuge.

Moldova, *1991*

This country became independent of the USSR in 1991; it sits next to Romania and has remained a communist state. They are the poorest country in Europe. Russian forces have remained on the land in the east, supporting a separatist group made up of Ukrainians and Russians, causing unrest in the country. The only resource they have is agriculture so they import everything else (gas, electric, phones, etc.) from Russia. They are working on privatizing enterprise.

Monaco, *1419*

This small country in the south of France was originally built as a fortress. It's the second smallest country in the world with a great, mild climate. Their income is tourism and gambling, which opened up after the railway system from France was brought into the area. They used to be impoverished but gambling has made them wealthy. They have no income tax and do not publish their financial state.

Mongolia, *1921*

In the 13th century the Mongols became famous because of Genghis Khan who brutally took over a great deal of Europe. After he died they fell under China's rule until they became independent. The country went from communist to democratic in 1990, but then in 2000 the former communist rulers won the election. They have a lot of natural resources, but because of dependence on Russia (the only country they buy from), China (the only country they sell to), natural disasters and political infighting, they have not benefited from the resources. They have begun privatizing and joined the WTO in 1999.

Montenegro, 2006

This was once known as the Kingdom of Serbs and was built and inhabited by Croats and Slovenes, two different cultures. In 1929, it changed its name to Yugoslavia. During WWII, Germany took over the country with great difficulty because the two different groups that lived in the country fought against the Germans but also ended up going into a civil war and fighting against each other. Eventually, Germany did take over the country and it actually became the first place where a concentration camp was built. After WWII, a communist dictator named Tito took over the country until his death in 1980. After his death, Yugoslavia separated out into ethnic areas. By 1992, these areas became the independent states of Slovenia, Croatia, Macedonia, Bosnia and Herzegovina. Initially, these independent states had their government heads meet routinely to try to work out economic and border issues, but the remaining lands pulled themselves together and called themselves the Federal Republic of Yugoslavia. They were run by Serbs and led by a violent dictator called Milosevic who began a civil war. He called upon Serbs living in all the different states to rise up and overtake or kill all non-Serbs so the country could be one again; it was to be called Greater Serbia. Initially, the UN and the world did not get involved with this conflict. Neighboring countries would not allow refugees to enter. After about two years, the severity of the brutality of what was happening became known and the UN got involved. Millions of non-Serbs were tortured, killed and kept in concentration camps. Initially, this country was part of Serbia, and together they held on to the idea of a united country and called themselves the Federal Republic of Yugoslavia. In 2003, it became Serbia and Montenegro, but in 2006 Montenegro separated itself out, and in doing so tried to separate itself from the Serbs and the war. At this time, there are no statistics available.

Morocco, 1956

This sits in Northern Africa and in 788 the Arabs had conquered Africa, with this area becoming especially powerful. Its then-leadership successfully fought off multiple attempts at outside reigns. But in 1860

Spain took over this area, eventually losing it to France in 1912, which brought them into independence. Today they have border disputes with Western Sahara that are still not resolved. Morocco overtook most of Western Sahara in 1970. They started to modernize their government in 1990. In 2002, and then again in 2006, they held elections. They are a newly developing country trying to get used to reducing spending and spreading the wealth around. But for now the people are in poverty, uneducated and have lots of debt. The IMF and World Bank are working with them to upgrade their infrastructure.

Mozambique, 1975

This country sits on the edge of South Africa and depends on them for financial aid. They have been in drought and a long civil war. They tried to form a constitution in 1989 but did not find peace until 1992 when the UN stepped in to form a treaty. This was the world's poorest country, but in recent years they have started to build an economy. They still rely on outside aid to stay alive. They have a huge death rate due to AIDS.

Navassa Island, 1857

This uninhabited Caribbean island next to Haiti was first used for mining. Today it is a wildlife refuge and is often used for scientific expeditions.

Namibia, 1990

This recently separated itself off from South Africa after a civil war that lasted from 1966 to 1988. They are the fourth largest exporter of minerals and the fifth largest uranium site in the world (uranium among other things makes nuclear weapons). Although they have a good-sized national income, the population does not see it and they live in abject poverty, eating what they can grow. They have one of the largest AIDS populations on the planet. The country is looking to privatize business and increase its standard of living.

Nauru, 1968

This is the world's smallest independent republic. It's a small island in the Pacific that actually has an unknown history as to where its people originated as they have a dialect like no other county. Initially, Germany annexed them in 1888, then Australia, and in WWII, a brutal invasion by Japan almost destroyed these people. The UN took over after the war, helped them rebuild and find independence. They mine and export phosphate. They are considered a third world country and the phosphate is drying up. They have been borrowing heavily and are trying to set up offshore accounts. At present, Australia is financially taking care of this small group of people, but the cost is high.

Nepal, *1768*

This country sits between China and India. They ended a complete monarchy state in 1951 and began a democracy within a monarchy in 1990. In 1996, an insurgent group (the Maoist) almost brought down the regime. A cease-fire was negotiated, but then broke down in 2003. In 2001, the crown prince massacred 10 members of his family, including the king and queen, before taking his own life. In 2002, the new king dismissed his prime minister for "incompetence" because, among other things they dissolved the elected parliament which weakened the government, which in turn was why the Maoist cease-fire broke down. At first the new king brought back the last elected prime minister, but by 2005 the insurgency was so bad that the king formally dissolved the government, declared a state of emergency, imprisoned party leaders and took over as ruling power of the country. In 2006, after seven weeks of intense protest by the Maoist party, the king allowed the parliament to reopen and new constitution elections were to be held in 2007. They have a lot of refugees living on the land, mostly Bhutanese who have fled a civil war. The UN pays for their housing at this time. This is one of the poorest countries (over one third of the population is in abject poverty and starving) with poor education and economy. Agriculture and the making of carpets is their biggest income. They would like to increase tourism, but the country is unstable.

Netherlands, *1815*

In the 1500s, this country was the leading seafaring commercial power. After 20 years of French occupation they finally obtained their independence. It sits next to Germany and was brutalized in WWII; because of that, they founded NATO, then the EC/EU. They are very politically active and have a large, prosperous, open economy.

New Caledonia, *1853*

This small island is east of Australia and was initially settled by both Britain and France. Eventually France took full possession and used it as a penal colony for four decades. In the 1980s and early 1990s, the country began its process for independence. In 2013, this country should become independent of France.

New Zealand, *1907*

These are two islands next to Australia that have been inhabited by the island natives, called Maori, since 800 AD. In 1840, the chieftains gave over territorial rights to Britain. The British colonized through a few settlements, then a series of land wars wiped out the natives. The New Zealand colonists became independent of Britain in 1907. The government started reforms in the 80s to open up their economy. Like Australia, their economy follows the U.S. by about six months.

Nicaragua, *1821*

By 1978, this country, which sits in Central America between the Caribbean and Pacific Ocean, was seen as completely corrupt. Guerrillas known as Sandinistas took over the country by 1979. They assisted the rebels in neighboring El Salvador, a country which had U.S. interests with the U.S. backing anti-Sandinista guerrillas throughout the entire 80s. Free elections were held in the 90s, but the Sandinista guerrillas were not defeated until 2001. But in 2006, the Sandinistan former president was overwhelmingly re-elected. The country has also been hit hard by hurricanes. Their economy is based on illegal drugs and they live in poverty. International aid helps keep the people alive, but they have a long way to go.

Niger, *1960*

This country in Western Africa became independent of France, but then was under military rule for 31 years. They held their first elections in 1993, which was followed by intense political infighting; this kept the government frozen the entire time. In 1996, a coup by Colonel Bare took over, and then another coup happened in 1999, killing off Colonel Bare. The new government restored democratic rule, with the president being re-elected again in 2004. They struggle with severe depression, terrible education due to the almost total lack of governmental infrastructure, seasonal severe drought and AIDS. In 1999, the World Bank gave them $105 million to build their country. There is still infighting and unrest. They have very few resources and are rated last in the UN human developmental fund.

Nigeria, *1960*

After gaining independence from Britain, this African country spent 16 years under a dictatorship. In 1999, they made the transition to civilian government. They have had the same president since. The country is impoverished. They have ethnic and religious differences within the people; the culture is split. They used to be a petroleum-based economy, but this has dried up and the revenues are gone due to the previous government. They are still oil-rich but are unable to access the oil. The IMF gave them a $1 billion credit in 2000, but in 2002 they had to pull out of the deal and forgo the money after failing to make some basic reforms. In 2003, the government started to turn things around, and in 2005 they paid off $30 billion of a $36 billion debt. They are the most populated African country and have over 250 different ethnic groups.

Niue, *1974*

This small island in the South Pacific was part of the Cook Islands and has less than 2,000 people on it. The population continues to fall as people continue to emigrate to New Zealand. It is a remote island that has language differences even between its own inhabitants. It has very few resources and requires New Zealand to keep it financially sound. It has basically no industrialized economy.

North Korea, *1945*

After WWII, Korea was split into North Korea and South Korea. The north went under communistic rule and the south under western influence. This holds the world's most isolated large economy and community. It is military-run; the people rarely if ever are exposed to outside influence, including South Korea. The present ruler took over for his father, who ruled it from its inception until his death in 1994, but was actually ruling the country since 1980. His father was a poor leader, letting industry and economy fall. He severely mismanaged the country. He demonized the U.S., telling his people that it was the ultimate threat to their country. Propaganda is strong; for example, only the ruler's picture is displayed everywhere, no economic advertisements are allowed. A radio station playing propaganda is in everyone's home, and they are not allowed to turn it off. Due to their isolation, they do not trade, so they can't even get basic things like fertilizer for their soil, which has deteriorated and is unable to grow crops. Since 1990 the people have been starving. Food aid has been dropped since 1995, but the country refuses to let anyone inside. Any money the government does get goes to military, which has over 1 million soldiers. They claim they are capable of building a nuclear bomb and will use it against the U.S. and South Korea, as one of their goals is to unite Korea again. In 2006, it tested ballistic missiles, and then in October of 2006 it tested a nuclear weapon. North Korea, along with China, U.S., Japan, Russia and South Korea, had been in talks (known as the Six-Party Talks), but North Korea dropped out in anger over the other countries wanting them to stop their program. Aid to the country was stopped, and in 2006 they announced they would return to the talks in 2007.

Northern Mariana Islands, 1975

This is a set of small tropical islands in the north pacific between Hawaii and the Philippines that used to be a UN Trust Territory. In the 1970s, they chose not to become an independent country and instead started negotiations with the U.S. to become a territory. Fifty percent of its economy is tourism, predominately Japanese, which is at minimum a half million dollars a year. They have many ranches (including cattle ranches) on the island with Chinese workers, and ship meat and agriculture to the U.S.

Norway, 1905

For two centuries Europe was raided by the Vikings. In 994 AD, King Tryggvason brought Christianity to Europe, which ended the Viking rule. This entire area was converged into the Norwegian Kingdom over a few decades. In 1397, Norway was absorbed into Denmark for several centuries, then Sweden tried to absorb them and they resisted. Eventually Sweden overtook them, but then reforms started going throughout Europe and they were given their independence. They claimed neutrality in both World Wars but were overtaken in WWII. After five years they abandoned "neutrality" and joined NATO in fighting back. In the 60s, oil was discovered offshore. Today they have a high welfare system; along with trying to decrease this, they are trying to build an economy other than oil. At present they are the third largest exporter of oil. They declined admission to the EU.

Oman, *1615*

This country sits next to Saudi Arabia and has a long history of prosperity in trade. In the 1800s, they signed a series of treaties with Britain and became very dependent on them. The present Sultan overthrew his father for reign in 1970. Since then, he has modernized the country while maintaining good relations with both the UK and the Arab world. They joined the WTO in 2001 and continue to become a liberated country.

Pacific Ocean

This is the world's largest of the five oceans. It sits between Australia and the Western Hemisphere. It is 15 times the size of the U.S. and 28% of the global surface. It presently has the largest amount of endangered species and pollution because it contains the busiest ports. In 1996, 60% of the world's fish came from this ocean. There is also a problem with the exportation of offshore oil and gas reserves from the U.S.

Pakistan, *1947*

In 1947, India (then British-held), which was predominately Hindu, divided off Pakistan (predominately Muslim) into its own two-part country (after severe infighting) called East and West Pakistan. India never fully accepted this, and another war broke out in 1971 which resulted in East Pakistan becoming its own country (Bangladesh). India and Pakistan remain in conflict even today; essentially, they never stopped fighting. In 1998, India announced it was building a nuclear weapon to use against Pakistan; within six months, Pakistan said it too was building its own nuclear weapon. In 1999, there was a military take-over of the government, which actually helped because the new government managed to pay back some international loans and started to create an economy. The people are ignorant and impoverished with corrupt agencies. The country has very little resources, but does not receive as much aid as it would like because of its unstable political situation and previous refusal to work with humanitarian organizations. This country also borders Afghanistan, and it's believed that al-Qaeda leader Osama bin Laden is living inside the borders of this country in the mountain range.

Palmyra Atoll, *1959*

This series of small volcanic islands was claimed by Hawaii, and then the U.S. It is a nature conservatory and a national wildlife refuge.

Palua, *1994*

This small island close to the Philippines was held by the UN in trust under U.S. administration until 1978. Then the cluster of islands around Palua became the Micronesian Islands, but they opted for independence. Their economy is tourism, fishing and agriculture. They do twice as much tourism as the Philippines, and are hoping this grows as people travel to the Pacific more.

Panama, *1903*

The U.S. helped this country become independent from Columbia back in 1903 in exchange for allowing a canal to be built. The Panama Canal was built between 1904 and 1914 and signed over to the U.S. in 1977 with an agreement that the U.S. would own the canal by 1999. In 1998, the U.S. helped depose the dictator Manuel Noriega. In 1999, the U.S. did not take the canal, but rather gave it back to Panama along with all the military bases and surrounding land the U.S. owned there. The canal, along with other service-oriented business like insurance, ports and flag registry, is this country's main income. In 2006, they approved a plan to expand the canal (doubling its size) to be completed by 2014-15. Their economy is not all that strong and many citizens remain impoverished.

Papua New Guinea, *1975*

This country sits between Australia and Indonesia. The physical island is called New Guinea, but it is divided into two countries: Indonesia and Papua New Guinea. In 1997, they ended a nine-year war with the indigenous people of the main island and a smaller island called Bougainville; over 20,000 people were killed. Both islands were being mined by Australia when unrest regarding Australia's control, mining profits and abuse erupted into civil war. Today they are trying to maintain peace, heal the wounds of civil war and build a relationship with Australia for a proposed pipeline.

Paracel Islands, *1932*

This is a series of 130 small coral islands and reefs claimed by two countries. The surrounding waters are productive fishing grounds with potential oil reserves. Since 1974, China has occupied the Paracel Islands. They are in dispute. In 1997, China announced plans to open the islands for tourism, but nothing has come of this at present.

Paraguay, *1811*

This country sits next to Brazil and has a long history of war; at one point it lost two thirds of its population to war. In 1989, a 35-year military government was overthrown and they have held open elections since. They still have frequent internal breakouts of war. They do a lot of import/ export with their neighbors, but they lack infrastructure. Most people live on what they can grow and make.

Peru, *1821*

They have a history of having perhaps the oldest recorded Indian civilization (this used to be part of Spain). They became a democratic state in 1980 after two decades of military rule. The president in the 90s turned around an impoverished economy and helped limit the severe guerilla activity they had, but he gradually became a dictator himself, and in 2000 he was ousted by their congress (with some international help). This country has survived on foreign investment and money from the World Bank. They were also devastated by El Nino. They are in a strong transition period and still have problems with guerrilla activity, corruption and drug trade.

Philippines, *1946*

After becoming independent from the U.S. (which took over the islands from the Japanese in 1946, then freed the islands), they fell under the rule of Ferdinand Marcos for 21 years before the people exiled him in 1986. Multiple presidents were elected then deposed in multiple coups. In 1992, the U.S. closed the last of its military bases here. In 2001, their Supreme Court elected a president, but there was so much uprising from the people that the presidency went to the vice-president,. In 2004, they elected a president for a six-year term and he's still in office. The southern area is presently being invaded by a Muslim population, and the country is trying to stop this invasion. Overall, the country is home to three major international terrorist groups. Their infrastructure and economy is in poor shape and their economy presently depends on trade with the U.S. and Japan.

Pitcairn Island, *1767*

This small Pacific island near New Zealand was the first territory claimed by Britain in the Pacific, and it is the last territory in the Pacific that they hold. It only has 45 people living on the island. Their major source of income is selling postage stamps to collectors and handcrafts to passing ships. The inhabitants live off of fertile land and lots of fresh fruit.

Poland, *1918*

This is one of the world's ancient nations; formed in the 10th century, it gained great power in the 16th century. Like many European nations, in the next few years the aristocracy and gentry created weakness within the nation, and eventually the country broke up into several lands, including Russia and Austria. Poland gained its independence in 1918, but was overrun in WWII by both the Germans and Russia who used it as a satellite. The country was very devastated in the war. In the 80s, the labor party called the "Solidarity Party" became so strong it took over the country in 1990. During the 90s, this party worked hard to increase the economy which had been very impoverished. In 2001, the Solidarity Party was overwhelmingly defeated and the government became more democratic. In 1999, they joined NATO, and then the EU in 2004. Their infrastructure had declined, but in recent years it has increased and they have become a large financial part of Europe.

Portugal, *1143*

This used to be called the Kingdom of Portugal, and in the 15th and 16th centuries it was very powerful. In 1755, it was hit with a major earthquake. This was followed by an occupation during the Napoleonic wars. They lost much of their wealth, status and land. In 1910, a revolution deposed their longstanding monarchy, but then they spent six years under different repressive governments. In 1974, a military coup installed democratic reforms. The following year, Portugal gave independence to all of its African-held nations, became a founding member of NATO and the EU.

Puerto Rico, *1493*

In 1493, this small Caribbean island was claimed by the Spanish following Columbus' voyage to the Americas. The island was filled with Aboriginal people. They endured 400 years of colonial war and the indigenous population was nearly exterminated. The island was filled with African slave labor. After the Spanish-American war, Puerto Ricans were granted U.S. citizenship in 1917. In 1952, they created their own constitution. In 1998, voters chose to stay a territory of the U.S. Since the 1950s, U.S. firms have invested heavily in Puerto Rico. They have a large amount of industry, including dairy production and tourism.

Qatar, *1971*

This country sits right next to Saudi Arabia and prior to its independence from Britain, harvesting pearls was its income. Now oil and gas bring in large revenue. This country was ruled by the Al-Thani family since the 1800s, but in 1995 the son overthrew the father to rule, and since income has increased and he stopped border disputes with neighboring countries.

Reunion, *1513*

The Portuguese initially discovered this uninhabited island off of southern Africa. Between the 17th and the 19th century, the French immigrated to the island along with Africans, Chinese, Malays and Malabar Indians, which gave the island its ethnic mix. This used to be a stopover for East Indies trade routes, but then in 1869 the Suez Canal opened and people no longer stopped on the island. Today, sugar cane is their major export and the government is trying to start tourism. There is a distinct financial gap between the wealthy whites and the very poor non-whites causing a lot of tension on the island. In 1991, there were violent and bloody riots that exposed this problem.

Romania, *1877/1991*

This is one of the many countries formed after the Ottoman Turks' reign was over, merging two territories to become Romania in 1877. During WWI, they merged Transylvania into their country, but in 1947 they became occupied by Russia and were under their rule until 1991 when the USSR fell apart. The country was under a local communist dictator from 1980 to 1989 who was cruel and sadistic. He was overthrown by another communist dictator who was in office until 1996, when he was overthrown. Currently the government is democratic but struggling after years of violence and oppression. The country is very poor; its income is at least 40% less than other European countries. In 2007, it was able to join the EU.

Russia, *1991*

Like many countries, this evolved from what was formerly the USSR. From 1924 to 1953, a brutal dictator named Stalin amassed a lot of land later to be known as the USSR. He killed over 10 million of his own people. He was overthrown, but communism had been born. The country suffered horrible economy and militant rule until the late 80s when Mikhail Gorbachev took over and brought glasnost (openness) and perestroika (restructuring). He initially tried to modernize communism but this backfired and the USSR splintered, mainly back into the (15) countries that existed before the USSR took over. Since then, it has struggled to form a democracy. The country has had a really hard time financially; the people had been very poor without an established modern economy. They're a large country, but much of the land is unusable. Eighty percent of their economy is exported oil, gas and timber. Their own infrastructure is weak, they are subject to poor internal industry, corruption (mafia-like groups often overtake entire areas) and a weak legal system. The new president came in young and energized, but within a few years Putin became known as controlling, including controlling the media. Many people who stood up to Putin were imprisoned. The economy has become stronger in the last fear years. One of their very serious problems is an area called Chechnya where Russian guerillas have taken hold and still plan to overthrow the country. Over the past few years, the Chechen rebels have done some horrific terrorist acts, especially against children. They took over a theatre that was doing a play for children, and hundreds died. Then they took over a school, also killing hundreds; both attacks were taped as part of the terrorists' fear-based plot.

Rwanda, 1962

In 1959, the ethnic group Hutu (which held the majority of the population) overthrew the Tutsi king. Thousands were killed, and over 150,000 were driven out to neighboring countries. The children of the exiled Tutsi grew up and formed a rebel group called the Rwandan Patriotic Front and in 1990 they went to war to take back their country. From 1990 to 1994 the genocide of millions of Hutus took place; most died within a brutal six-month period, and in one month alone at the beginning of the war, 800,000 were killed by hand-held machetes. It was one of the most violent civil wars in history. Most of the deaths were done by machete, with children stolen and taken into the Tutsi army to service the army men. Two million Hutus became refugees in neighboring lands. Since then, many Hutus have returned, but there is now a rebel Hutu group forming in a neighboring country. Also, since 1994, Rwanda went through two other wars with a neighboring country. The country is impoverished, emotionally brutalized, and a lot of anger and resentment remains between the two ethnic groups. They held their first elections in 1999, but they do not have a stable government, nor an infrastructure. This is a small country and is the most densely populated country in Africa. Neighbors who tortured neighbors live very close together. They have received enormous aid money, but they really have very little resources.

Saint Helena, *1502*

This small uninhabited island outside of Africa was first discovered by the Portuguese. The British took it over in the 18th century and colonized it. It's the place where Napoleon was exiled until his death. It used to be a trading port until the Suez Canal was built. Today, there is a U.S. auxiliary navy port and a meteorlogical station. There are 7,000 people living on the island, mainly subsidized by the UK.

St. Kitts and Nevis, *1983*

These two Caribbean islands became independent of Britain; sugar was their main economy until the 70s when tourism and offshore banking became large parts of the economy. Tourism is their main economy, but like many islands, it has fallen off since 9/11 and their economy is falling. In 1998, Nevis attempted to separate from St. Kitts unsuccessfully, but is still trying at present.

St. Lucia, *1979*

This Caribbean island became independent of Britain after Britain and France fought over the island 14 times; French is still the language spoken there. They export bananas and have offshore banking and tourism.

Saint Pierre and Miquelon, *1763*

This small North American island, not far from Canada, is the last remaining French territory in this area. There are less than 7,000 people on the island that survive through fishing and subsidies from the French economy. The government is hoping to build a tourism industry.

St. Vincent and the Grenadines, *1979*

These Caribbean islands became independent of Britain, but like its neighbor St. Lucia, Britain and France fought over the area for a full century. It is one large island with a series of about 20 smaller ones. Their economy is very poor; tourism is not that strong and agriculture is their only resource on land. They have offshore banking but with an unusual secrecy "law" that other governments are now looking into, which has caused money to be pulled out of their accounts.

Samoa, *1962*

This sits between Hawaii and New Zealand and used to be occupied by New Zealand, and then Germany. This is the first Polynesian country to become independent. They are traditionally dependent on aid and routinely get wiped out by tropical storms, but tourism is looking up. The country is starting to privatize business and their economy is starting to flow.

San Marino, *301 AD*

This is the third smallest country in Europe and neighbor to Italy. They claim to be the world's first republic after being founded by a Christian stonemason back in 301 AD. Their economy tends to follow Italy's. Tourism is 50% of their economy, with banking, electronics, apparel and ceramics making up the rest. They are fairly prosperous.

Sao Tome and Principe, *1975*

This West African island just held their first free elections in 1991. This island was filled with slaves even into the 20th century with sugar, cocoa and coffee plantations. They are still dependent on cocoa and have to import all of their goods. They are very poor and receiving aid ($200 million last year), but the island has potential for tourism and just discovered that they have oil offshore. In 1995 and in 2003, coup attempts to take over the government were unsuccessful, but the government has changed over a lot and remains unstable.

Saudi Arabia, *1932*

This was 13 provinces that became one country and the birth place of Islam. It holds Islam's two holiest shrines (Mecca and Medina). In the 1930s, oil was discovered and the country changed and became very financially powerful in the worlds economy. They took in the Kuwait refugees along with their royal family when it was invaded in 1990. They also allowed foreign troops, mainly American, to stay. Long after Kuwait was resolved, American troops and multiple business endeavors remained in Saudi, creating tension and public complaints until they left in 2003.

Terrorist attacks (against U.S. military and civilians) in 2003 within Saudi brought out an internal struggle that the country was already having with terrorists; this is the home of Osama bin Laden. This country is a mixture of the very ancient and the very modernized. For example, the present king held elections in 2005 for half the members of municipal (local) councils, yet appointed the other half. They depend on oil for the economy, holding 25% of the known world's oil reserves. They're becoming over-populated and have water issues. In 1999, they started the process of privatizing their economy to some degree and recently joined the WTO. They have strong political and business ties to the U.S., but also remain well connected with their neighboring Arab countries.

Serbia, *1918*

This was once know as the Kingdom of Serbs and was built and inhabited by Croats and Slovenes, two different cultures. In 1929, it changed its name to Yugoslavia. During WWII, Germany took over the country with great difficulty because the two different groups that lived in the country fought against the Germans but also ended up going into a civil war and fighting against each other. Eventually, Germany did take over the country and it actually became the first place where a concentration camp was built. After WWII, a communist dictator named Tito took over the country until his death in 1980. After his death, Yugoslavia separated out into ethnic areas. By 1992, these areas became the independent states of Slovenia, Croatia, Macedonia, Bosnia and Herzegovina. Initially, these independent states had their government heads meet routinely to try to work out economic and border issues, but the remaining lands pulled themselves together and called themselves the Federal Republic of Yugoslavia. They were run by Serbs and led by a violent dictator called Milosevic who began a civil war. He called upon Serbs living in all the different states to rise up and overtake or kill all non-Serbs so the country could be one again; it was to be called Greater Serbia. Initially, the UN and the world did not get involved with this conflict. Neighboring countries would not allow refugees to enter. After about two years, the severity of the brutality of what was happening became known and the UN got involved. Millions of non-Serbs were tortured, killed and kept in concentration camps. In 1998, this country went through another insurgence of ethnic fighting that resulted in the loss of land and the changing of the government. In 2004, and again in 2006, they had riots in their capital. They are trying to put the government back together and have rejoined the UN. The neighboring countries, where the Serbs committed such atrocities, are in the process of suing and looking for justice for what was done.

Sierra Leone, 1961

This West African country sits next to Liberia and has been in civil war since 1971. Over two million of its people have fled to neighboring countries (one third of the population), and tens of thousands have died. The UN and World Bank have been in there for years. In 2002, the rebel forces were finally captured; now the goal is to establish a government and some kind of economy. The UN peacekeepers stayed until 2005. They established a UN Integrated Office to help establish a new government. In 2007, elections are going to be held to begin a new government body. This country basically lives off of outside help, and AIDS is killing off a large portion of their population.

Senegal, 1960

This African country tried to form together with their neighboring country Gambia in the 80s, but it didn't work. In 2000, they elected a new government after 40 years under the same reign. They have a chronic problem with a small separatist group that still clashes with their government; in 2004, the peace agreements became deadlocked. Despite this, they are actually a stable country when it comes to violence and government compared to many other African countries. In 1994, they started an intense economic reform including getting the country "fully connected to the Internet" which increased technology and education. Their economy is increasing but they have problems of urban violence, teenage gangs, inflation and unemployment.

Singapore, 1965

This country, a small island off of Malaysia, after achieving independence from Britain, became one of the wealthiest countries due to trade. They have the busiest ports, trading both eastern and western goods, a stable government and good relations internationally.

Slovakia, 1993

In 1918, this country joined with Czechs and formed Czechoslovakia. After WWII, they became part of the USSR, gaining independence after its collapse. In 1993, the Czechs and Slovaks peaceably split. They struggled economically with a persistent high unemployment rate until 2001 when their economy, based in outside banking and automotive industry, stabilized. At this time their banking and finances are held by outside sources, and they are still building an infrastructure. By 2004, they were able to join the EU and NATO.

Slovenia, *1991*

This is one of the countries that separated out of Yugoslavia and is doing well. They did not have as many losses as the other states that separated out of Serb-controlled Yugoslavia; when the former Yugoslavian principalities went into a bloody Serbian-based war in the mid-90s (the Serbs were trying to control and unite the country again), this country had separated out already and formed European ties, so they were not as vulnerable as other places like Bosnia. They were the wealthiest before the civil war, so they had a good infrastructure and cash flow after the war. They also have a strong democracy.

Solomon Islands, *1978*

These islands are in the South Pacific and were owned by Britain. They actually saw some of the heaviest fighting in WWII. They have a big problem with ethnic violence, government corruption and gangs. It became so bad that they sought help from Australia in 2003, which then sent in troops to disarm militia groups and restore order. They have to import most of their goods and are potentially going to lose things like oil, gas and telecommunications due to lack of paying their bills (they import these). In recent years, outside help has effectively helped them restore government and law and is starting to rebuild the country. The land is rich in unmined minerals.

Somalia, *1978*

This sits next to Ethiopia and used to be two separate provinces, one ruled by Britain, the other by Italy. In 1960, Britain withdrew, allowing the two to come together and form Somalia. Then in 1969, a violent coup brought in a strong socialist government that kept the country under some degree of stability for a few decades. In 1991, the regime was overthrown and the country has experienced infighting ever since. The north and south are basically split. The north declared independence, although they did not formalize this in any way, but due to their history with Britain, and both Russian and American military help, they had a stable infrastructure. Another group of lands (this would be like "states" in the U.S.) does not claim independence, but function separately and are called Puntland. In 1993, the UN went in (mainly in the South) for humanitarian aid initially, staying on to help Nation Build, but pulled out in 1995 after heavy casualties. The capital is Mogadishu, and in 1993 there were some violent battles for control here. This country is made up of several strong clans; an Islamic one run by Aideed took over the capital and forced Islam onto the people. The U.S. went in along with the UN. During the invasion, the U.S. retrieved some officials they were sent in to rescue, but one of their Black Hawk helicopters was shot down with an American soldier's body mutilated and paraded in front of the cameras all over the world. The U.S. pulled out of the effort, and soon after, so did the UN. The UN went back in around 2000 to help set up an interim government. In 2004, there were basically two governments set up: one getting ready to take over (TFA), and one Islamic one controlling most of the country (SCIC) and believed to have ties to al-Qaida. In 2006, Mogadishu was taken over by the TFA, backed by Ethiopian forces (which are backed by the U.S.), but the country is very unstable and Islamic-forced control of the people is still present.

South Africa, 1910

The Dutch and native Africans lived here until the British took over this country in 1803, after which most of the Dutch left. In the middle of the 1800s, diamonds and gold were discovered here in large numbers and the natives were subjugated to work in the mines. The remaining Dutch did go to war against this but were defeated (1899-1902). They became the "union" of South Africa and functioned under apartheid, which is the action of separating out people by race. British rule was dissolved in the 1990s and apartheid was finally dissolved when blacks, who had been under control, became rulers. The country still has race issues, huge unemployment, one of the largest AIDS populations, corruption, gang-like violence and poverty. On the other hand, they have large resources and potential for great wealth, but their infrastructure is weak.

South Georgia and the South Sandwich Islands, 1908

This set of islands sits off the tip of South America. In the early 19th century, it was used as a whaling station and has been used as a stop-off place for people crossing the Antarctic. There are no indigenous inhabitants. They have a large bird and seal population. They house scientific studies for Antarctic studies.

South Korea, *1945*

After WWII, Korea was split into North Korea and South Korea. The north went under communistic rule and the south under western influence. There was a Korean War (1950-1953), in which UN forces and the U.S. stepped in to help South Korea fight off North Korea. When a treaty was signed, South Korea had more land, and the land was richer than North Korea's. They were growing as a Western nation, until from 1997 to 1999 when their economy crashed; since then, they have been slowly coming back. In 2000, there was a summit between North and South Korea set up by Kim Dae-jung (who won the Nobel Peace Prize for doing this). He states he is committed to democracy and peace at all cost. In 2003, when the U.S. broke off all talks with North Korea, President Dae-jung was successful in talking with his counterpart. Import/export and external relations play a large part in their economy. There biggest threat is North Korea, which has missile and nuclear capability and wants to take over South Korea to put the whole country under communistic rule.

Southern Ocean

The entire Antarctic Ocean is divided into north and south by the area where the cold waters meet the warm waters. This point is referred to as the Antarctic Convergence, which fluctuates with seasons. This Southern Ocean flows in a circular motion around Antarctica. It wasn't until 2000 that the Antarctic Ocean was divided into north and south. The convergence point where warm water hits cold water creates a unique ecological system where plant life flourishes, which in turn allows for greater abundance of ocean animal life. Over recent years, the increased UV light has decreased the marine plant life by 15% and is damaging fish DNA. This ocean actually has over 12,000 visitors a year.

Spain, *1910*

This European country was a powerful world empire back in the 16th and 17th centuries, but it didn't keep up with change, mainly sea travel and trading so it fell behind France, Britain and Germany in both power and economy. During both WWI and WWII, Spain remained neutral, but they had been involved in their own civil war (1936-1939) that devastated the country. In 1975, they had a transfer of government over to a democracy after the long-ruling dictator died. They have just recently got their economy back on track, but they have a big problem with terrorism from a group called the Basque Fatherland and Liberty (BFL); this is similar to the IRA problem in Ireland. They have the highest unemployment rate of any country in the EU.

Spratly Islands, *1984*

These are 100 uninhabited islands in the South China Sea. They are being claimed by five different countries. Forty-five of the islands are occupied by small numbers of military sources from China, Malaysia, Philippines, Taiwan and Vietnam.

Sri Lanka, *1948*

This was inhabited in 6th century BC, probably from people coming down from India. Buddhism was introduced and then a "great civilization" developed from 200 BC to 1000 AD. In the 14th century, they were overtaken by an Indian civilization that was building its own dynasty. By the 16th century the Portuguese controlled them; in the 17th century the Dutch ruled. The Dutch lost it to the British (who named it Ceylon), and they had it until 1815. It achieved independence in 1948 and changed its name in 1972. They have two parties: Tamil separatists and the Sinhalese majority. They have been in an internal ethnic war since 1980. Tens of thousands have died. In 2002, Norway brokered a peace deal that fell through in 2006, and fighting resumed. They live off of exporting textiles, but in the last two years their previously strong economy is falling because of the persistent warring.

Sudan, *1956*

From 1956 (when they became independent of Britain) until now they have been in civil war, with the exception of 10 years (1972-1982). The war is between the Arab/Muslims in the north and the African/non-Muslims in the south. Over two million have died, four million live outside the country as refugees, and two million more are displaced within the country, most famously in the Darfur region where they are raped, killed and tortured literally daily in "international" refugee camps. These are poorly (if at all) protected due to the refusal of the controlling northern government, which refuses help for these refugees because unofficially they are the ones that made them refugees. Because these people are still within the Sudan borders, if the UN or any other country wants to forcibly help the refugees, they have to technically invade the country. There are months when 10,000 refugees are supposedly killed at a time; of the two million internally displaced, 400,000 are now dead. At present, there is much press given to this long-standing tragedy because it is considered another humanitarian disaster, like Rwanda and Bosnia that happened without any outside force coming in and stopping it. Famine has become a severe problem because of war. In 1999, they began exporting crude oil, but owe over $25 billion to international organizations that have brought money into the country. They are unstable but trying to form an economy and unified government.

Suriname, 1975

This country sits next to Brazil and has gone through several governments. It was originally explored by the Spaniards (16th century), then the British, and then the Dutch, who eventually abolished slavery and brought in workers from India and Java. Five years after gaining independence, they were overthrown by a militia group that ruled until 1989, when international forces came in and basically forced them to have democratic elections. In 1990, the militia overtook the country again. In 1991, the elected government took back power and has ruled ever since. There income was based on mining minerals until 2004 when offshore oil production began.

Svalbard, 12th century

Norway discovered this series of islands off of Northern Europe in the 12th century and used it as an international whaling base. It wasn't until the 1920s that was considered a formal territory. There are about 2,000 people living on the larger island involved in coal mining. Otherwise it is completely dependent on Norway for all goods.

Swaziland, 1968

This country sits next to South Africa and was once under British control. Student and labor uprising in the early 90s have forced the autocratic monarchy to start to accept some democratic change, but the people are still oppressed. They have the highest AIDS rate in the world. They had diamond mines that are now used up; the country suffers from drought and overuse of its lands. They rely heavily on South Africa for money.

Sweden, *1523*

They were a military power in the 17th century, but refused to participate in any war for over two centuries. They had a capitalist economy until 1990 when high unemployment forced them to change their ways. They still have one of the best economies in the world with consistent government surplus. They consider themselves "neutral" and did not participate in either world wars, but avoided being invaded by having a heavy military force at the borders. It is mandatory for the individual households to be armed and ready to protect the borders.

Switzerland, *1499*

This was originally formed in 1291, but was under Holy Empire Rule until its independence. Strong ties with the UN are historically based on economics and banking. They have worked at integrating Europe. Though they verbalize commitment to the UN and most international organizations, they claim to be "neutral" and will not physically involve themselves in anything political or humanitarian, including refusing to be actively involved in either WWI or WWII. It wasn't until 2002 that they even joined the UN. They have a large international banking industry.

Syria, *1946*

This Middle Eastern country was once part of the Ottoman Empire; most recently it was held by France until its independence. It sits next to Israel, and in 1967 they had a war and lost some of their land to Israel, specifically land just south of Lebanon. Since 1976 they have had troops in southern Lebanon (also a neighbor to Israel), supposedly to help maintain peace, but Israel has said it's to have a launching place to take back the land. In 2005 those troops were withdrawn. They have a long history of wars, even within the Arab community. They have a lot of economic problems including unusable water. They are just starting to privatize some industry, like banks, but this will take years. At this time, the economy is failing due to holding on to old ways and government control.

Taiwan, *1947*

This country is an island between China and Japan and has been inhabited for over 30,000 years. Many cultures found this island on their way to trade with Japan, including the Dutch in 1624, who established a society that included an orphanage (very rare) and taught their language to the natives. The Spanish spent years here on the north side of the island, but were driven out by the Dutch. Even the French settled here for a while. The Dutch were driven out in 1662 by Fujian, a part of China. The person who drove out the Dutch was married to a Japanese woman. After that, this country went back and forth between Japan and China until they won independence, which is disputed by China. After WWII, the Chinese ROC (military) occupied Taiwan. In 1949, China lost its own civil war to the Communist Party, and the former ruler (ROC) went to Taiwan. 1.3 million Chinese refugees fled to Taiwan. They went under communist rule until 2000 when they had the government transferred over to a democracy; it was a long slow transition without violence. They still have issues with China, including potentially going back under China's rule, and not being recognized by China as an independent country. Financially they are capitalist and do a lot of exporting; they also finance a lot for China.

Tajikistan, *1991*

This is another country that came out of the USSR only to go into a five-year civil war. A peace agreement was reached in 1997 but not implemented until 2000. They still have some fighting, even publicly out in streets. Cotton is their biggest crop, but their infrastructure is weak, the government is new and they need to recover from their civil war. They're seeking entry into the WTO and NATO. They have received over $300 million from Russia, and several more millions from other countries. This includes the U.S., which is spending $36 million on a bridge; they sit next to Afghanistan and the U.S. is linking a bridge between the two countries.

Tanzania, *1964*

This sits next to Kenya and is the result of merging two nations, Zanzibar and Tanganyika, after gaining independence from Britain. They had their first democratic elections in 1995, which were considered contentious and the outcome was questionable. This is one of the poorest countries in the world. They receive significant amounts of aid money. They have some natural resources of gold, natural gas and minerals, but their government is weak with no real infrastructure yet formed.

Thailand, *1238*

This country was known as Siam until 1939. They are the only Southeast Asian country to never have been taken over. Aligned with Japan during WWII, they became a U.S. ally afterwards. They had a high economic growth from 1985 to 1995, but then had a financial crisis in 1997, which uncovered government instability. They do a lot of exporting for their economy. Presently, Thailand's southern lands have been slowly invaded by a Muslim group that are coming over from neighboring Malaysia and have gotten a good foothold among the locals.

Togo, *1960*

This country is in Africa and is under military rule, which for many years was considered to be led by one of the most brutal dictators. They are under fire from international groups for human rights abuse and have a lot of political unrest. Due to severe abuse, most NGOs refuse to give aid, but the EU did initiate some aid in 2004. They are poor, isolated and the people have no say. They are the fourth largest producer of phosphate. In 2005, the son of the previous dictator took control after his father's death and held "elections" that solidified his rule. This country must import even basic products. They are supported by the IMF and World Bank.

Tokelau, *1840*

This country is made up of three small volcanic islands in the South Pacific that were originally settled by Polynesian immigrants, then taken over by the British in 1889. Then they were transferred to New Zealand in 1925. There are only three small villages on one island with less than 1,000 people, and they rely on New Zealand for their goods.

Tonga, *1970*

This south pacific island was dubbed the "friendly island" and remains the only monarchy in the area. They're also unique because they never lost their indigenous way of ruling. They were part of the Polynesian Kingdom in 1845, a British protectorate in 1900, and then became independent. They are basically stable, export a lot of crops and have a strong tourist base from New Zealand.

Trinidad and Tobago, *1962*

These islands are in the Caribbean and are probably the most prosperous because of oil, natural gas exports and tourism. They were colonized by the British in the early 19th century, but when slavery was abolished their sugar industry took the economy downward. They brought in contract workers from India and added on cocoa production. In 1910, oil was discovered on Trinidad.

Tromelin Island, *1776*

This uninhabited island is in the Indian Ocean off of South Africa. It was first discovered by the French before being turned over to Reunion. It is being disputed by Mauritius, and at present the only thing on it is a meteorological station.

Tunisia, *1956*

The French and Italians fought for this land, with the French winning in 1881. After WWI, this country started seeking independence. The first president lasted 31 years (through the 80s); he suppressed fundamental Islam and gave equal rights to women, the only Arab country to do so. They have a diverse economy, but the government still controls most of it. The country is very open in some areas, but politically they are a one-party country. They continue to modernize, have a diverse economy instead of just relying on one thing, and have joined the EU.

Turks and Caicos, *1962*

Prior to 1962, these were part of the Jamaican islands in the Caribbean. They separated off, and the governor of the Bahamas oversaw these islands as well. The Bahamas became independent of Britain in 1973, but these islands remained part of British rule. In 1982, they were going to declare independence, but chose to remain a territory of Britain. Their economy is based on tourism and offshore banking.

Turkey, *1923*

This country was one of many that formed after the fall of the Ottoman Empire. In the 1950s, democracy replaced the one-party system that had always ruled the country, but by the 1960s, the Democratic Party had fractured with multiple groups taking over. Three coups were attempted between 1960 and 1980, mostly by Islamic groups trying to take over. In 1974, Greece tried to take over this country, so Turkey took part of the Greek island of Cypress, which to this day only Turkey recognizes as their territory. They still have a difficult relationship. In 1984, a separatist group tried to take over the southeast section of the country and create Kurdistan; they failed, but their terrorist attacks were brutal, killing over 30,000 people until 1999 when the insurgents withdrew and went into Iraq instead to take over the northern part of that country. There are still about 5,000 separatists in northern Turkey, similar to the IRA. The country is a mix between old world and new. They have tried to join the EU under great protest from most of its members and are considered an "associate" member instead. They have to increase their democracy, economy and human rights practices before joining. Clothing and textiles are their biggest industry.

Turkmenistan, 1991

This country sits next to Iran and is one of the countries that became independent after the fall of the USSR, where it had been annexed since 1924. The country was under dominating control until the ruler died in 2006. This is the first elected president. They remain an impoverished country although they have a strong natural gas supply they could use, but the previous ruler didn't want to work with any outside communities. Today they access that supply and are looking to break Russia's pipeline monopoly by developing an alternative petroleum transportation route.

Tuvalu, 1978

These are a series of islands around Hawaii, part of the multiple Polynesian islands. They separated off from Britain and the Micronesian islands. They have no basic income; Australia set up a trust fund many years ago for this country and they have had good financial success managing it. The U.S. also spends $9 million a year on fishing from this country. In 2000, they sold their line for area codes, specifically 900, to an Internet server company for $50 million along with the ".tv" domain extension.

Uganda, 1962

This land was marked out, or given delineated boundaries by British rule. They grouped together a large range of cultures and people to do this, which also meant a large amount of different ethnicities and languages. After they obtained their independence, these differences stopped the process of creating a working government and allowed the take-over by a dictator from 1971 to 1979, who tortured and killed approximately

300,000 people. Another dictator took over from 1980 to 1985, who killed about 100,000 more. During the 1990s, the government was trying to change from dictatorship to a governmental body. They have lots of natural resources like copper and coffee, and are trying to get their economy going, but long internal wars, their continued involvement in the Congo War, and a corrupt government keeps them suffering. They were recently given $1.3 billion in debt relief.

Ukraine, *1991*

In the 10th and 11th centuries, this was part of the most powerful European state. The Mongol invasion and internal strife caused their downfall. They became part of Lithuania, then Poland. They became Ukraine in the mid-17th century after defeating the Poles and held on to their state for 100 years before being absorbed by the Russian Empire in 1917. For three years afterwards, they regained their independence, but were brutally reconquered and forced to live in a famine state that killed eight million. During WWII, both the Russian and German armies killed another eight million. After the USSR fell, the state controlled the country, stopping any democratic attempts. In 2004, a very large peaceful protest followed an election (their first), and put Viktor Yushchenko in office. He became globally known for having an American wife, being very Western himself, and being physically poisoned during the election process. After obtaining office, his own democratic party splintered, and he lost the presidency to his rival. Ukraine has very fertile soil and produces one fourth of the Soviet agriculture. In 2006, they passed 20 new laws to prepare the country to join the WTO.

United Arab Emirates, *1971*

This country used to be part of something called The Trucial States of the Persian Gulf. Britain had certain control over these states, including defense and foreign affairs since the 19th century. In 1971, six of the states joined together and formed the United Arab Emirates. This is a very wealthy Middle Eastern country due to oil, and they have strong influence on the Arab countries surrounding them. They have the fourth highest income of any country in the world. (In 1973 they were one of the most impoverished countries in the world). They have a strong traditional Islamic culture. They have a dictatorship and have violated basic Human Rights laws. Over the last five years, the U.S. has gotten financially involved with this country, including things like attempting to sell the job of U.S. port security to them, and other government jobs. A version of NASCAR is held in this country. U.S. businesses are given tax-free exemptions. Five of the terrorists from 9/11 came out of this country.

United Kingdom, *10ᵗʰ century*

This country has a very long history, and for being so physically small they have had a lot of power in the world. There was a time when one quarter of the world was under British rule. By the early 20ᵗʰ century, the country lost a lot of power and land, especially after WWII. It is one of the five founding members of the UN and NATO. They focus on "a global approach to policy," and are presently under reforms for land they have in Scotland, Ireland and Wales. They are a frequent target of the IRA, a terrorist group out of Ireland that wants Britain to release the six counties they rule in the country. They have a strong economy, and though they helped create the EU, they chose to not be a part of the monetary system at this time. The majority of the energy they use, including oil, they produce. This is unusual; most countries import. They have a large social economy, which they are trying to reform due to monetary loss in this area. They also have a very liberal immigration policy, which has been internally criticized because of the influx of large numbers of Muslims, many found to have ties to terrorist groups. Since joining the U.S. in invading Iraq, this country has had multiple terrorist attacks from within by its own Muslim-based UK citizens.

United States, *1776*

This country was founded by the British, but the French, Spanish, Native Americans and Mexicans also lived on the land at the time. Initial settlers were either British rule or indentured servants. Eventually the indentured population rose up and defeated the British, then French, Spanish, Mexican and Native Americans to call the land their own. The country is physically large, yet the settlers walked and rode most of the land (which has both desert and mountains) to create a civilization all over the country. This became a powerful democracy that went through its own devastating civil war that split the north and south regarding slavery. The north won, but to this day there is an issue with unification. As of today, this is the most powerful country on the planet with high technology. 1994 to 2000 marked the country's greatest financial increase, along with decreased unemployment, low crime rate and low inflation. In 2001, this took a dramatic turn with increased unemployment, increased inflation and fear regarding safety after several outside terrorist attacks occurred on one day perpetrated by Islamic extremists. The country retaliated by invading two Muslim countries, one it turned out, illegally (Iraq), and the country remains imbedded in a bloody civil war that it created after deposing the dictator. It has an increasingly weak infrastructure, skyrocketing healthcare problems, increased cost of education, decreased trade agreements, aging population, stagnating family incomes, high external and internal debt, discourse with the UN, increasing hatred from countries outside of the U.S., and is still embroiled in two wars. The general public is also known for its apathy, which concerns other countries because of the level of power the country holds.

Uruguay, 1828

This South American country was originally founded by the Spanish and used as a strategic military site, then claimed by Argentina to use as a large commercial center. Then Brazil took it over, until it successfully fought for its independence three years later. The first president created a healthy government and economy, but then a huge Marxist guerrilla movement in the 60s caused the government to become a military state in 1973. In 1985, this was dissolved. In 2004, a leftist president won the election, ending 170 years of same-party rule. Their economy is exported agriculture. It's one of the more stable South American countries.

Uzbekistan, 1991

Another country made independent after the fall of the USSR, it was initially taken over in the late 19th century, and after WWI this country fought hard against Russian rule, but lost. They used to be dependent on cotton sales, but they have depleted their land and are running out of water. They're now focusing on petroleum. They also have an insurgence of Islamic aggression coming in from Afghanistan which has slowly taken over the country. They are known for government hostility, lack of human rights and aggression. Their economy, once flourishing, is very poor and the people are being put in bondage. The government was set to receive $185 million in aid, but they would not work with the IMF so the money was withdrawn. In 2002, they asked for the money, claiming they are ready to work with the international government.

Vanuatu, *1980*

These are a group of small islands between Hawaii and Australia that were initially colonized by many cultures (and called the Hebrides until 1980), leaving them with a complex and diverse language. Both the French and British settled here in 1906 and administered the islands until their independence. Their economy is fishing, agriculture and offshore banking. They have had four severe natural disasters in the last eight years. Concern about where the money is coming from in their offshore accounts is prompting other governments to look into their financing.

Venezuela, *1830*

This South American country was once part of Colombia. In the first half of the 20th century they were ruled by a military government that promoted the oil industry and social reform. They have been a democracy since 1959. The current president, elected in 1999, is losing support because of his strong globalization campaign, while at home the country is struggling with poverty and a destabilized social system. The military is growing in power, and they are having drug war problems along the border of Colombia. The people themselves have a large population of drug addicts, which has caused a decreased work force. They export petroleum but are very dependent on it and their market fluctuates and is unstable. They are also mining the rainforest without eco consideration and displacing the indigenous people that live there without compensation. Recently the president has formed bonds with other countries that consider themselves "enemies" of the U.S. At a recent UN address, he called the U.S. president the "devil" and "evil" while trying to get support to undermine trading and military relations with the U.S.

Vietnam, *1954*

This area of Southeast Asia was under French rule and called French Indonesia. After WWII they declared independence but remained under France until 1954. The country became divided when communist forces took control of the north in 1956. The U.S. sent "military aid" to the south until a cease-fire was reached in 1973. The U.S. pulled out, never acknowledging that there was a war. Two years later the north over took the south. The country remains communist and the economy struggles as the leaders resist any reform, like privatizing business. They are very poor and overpopulated and used to get support from the USSR before it collapsed. Internally they have multiple groups in unrest and protesting the government. In 2001, a U.S.-Vietnam trade agreement was signed. The U.S. has entered the country again, but this time to help create and support a legal economic system. For many in both the U.S. and Vietnam, this is very controversial.

Virgin Islands, 1917

This set of small islands in the Caribbean was discovered and divided into two territories in the 17th century: one English, one Danish. In 1917, the U.S. purchased the Danish portion. Tourism is the primary economy. The island sees over two million visitors, mostly U.S. citizens. One of the world's largest petroleum refineries is on the smaller island of St. Croix. They have suffered a lot of damage from recent hurricanes and tropical storms.

Wake Island, 1899

This island in the North Pacific was annexed by the U.S. to use for a cable station, and during WWII it held a strategically important naval base. There are not indigenous inhabitants and since 1974 the U.S. has used it as a stopover for fueling cargo planes.

Wallis and Futuna, 1842

This is a series of islands in the South Pacific Ocean between Hawaii and New Zealand that was originally discovered by the British and the Dutch in the 17th century. It was the French that declared it and became the protectorate in 1842. In 1959, the inhabitants voted to stay a territory of France. Their economy is based on small farming and they are heavily subsidized by the French government. There is currently about 16,000 people living on the island.

West Bank, 1948

This small area of land sits on the West Bank of the Jordan River in the Middle East. When the Ottoman Empire fell, this became part of British rule inside the country of Palestine. After WWII, many areas in the world had to redefine their boundaries. This also became an opportunity for many new countries to claim territory. This is what happened in 1948. The Israeli nation, which did not have formal international recognized land, claimed the areas within Palestine as the Israeli nation. There was a war called the Arab-Israeli War in 1948, which ended up with the formal establishment of Israel. Within Israel, two areas, the Gaza Strip and the West Bank, were not captured by Israel. The Gaza Strip went to Egypt and the West Bank went to Jordan. Both of these areas were occupied by Israeli citizens, claiming that they owned the land. Both areas have been in almost constant war since 1948. Jordan officially relinquished the West Bank in 1988, but Palestine has not. This would be like the city of Chicago, even though it is inside the state if Illinois, being claimed by Canada. For both the Israeli community and the Palestinian community, there are deep religious beliefs associated with the small piece of land, which is why neither one wants to give it up. Today, it is under Palestinian rule and Israel has agreed to withdraw, but as yet they have not.

Western Sahara, *1976*

Morocco annexed two thirds of the territory in 1976 and the rest in 1977. A guerilla war within the country lasted from 1979 to 1991 when the UN brokered a cease-fire. The UN is still working with this country on referendums and non-compliance. The country lacks rainfall. The people are nomadic. Most of their food must be imported. Morocco is exploring oil off the coast. The standard of living is very low and the people are impoverished. There are no usable statistics on the country, except the fact that there are about 250,000 people living here.

Yemen, *1990*

In 1918, this country became independent of the Ottoman Empire, but there was a north and south Yemen. A Marxist government took over the south in the 1960s, and much of the population fled to the north. For two decades, the north and south fought until they unified in 1990 as one country. In 1994, the south tried to secede again but was stopped. They are presently trying to agree on borders with Saudi Arabia. This has been one of the poorest Arab countries. They have just started producing oil and international organizations are in the country helping them with aid, money and infrastructure, but the country is unstable and civil war is still possible. There is also concern about terrorists being here.

Zambia, *1964*

This South African country was ruled by Britain in the 1920s until its independence. Copper mining was the strongest economy, started by the British. It began democratic elections in 1991 as their economy of copper export was failing. Even in 2001, the election system was corrupt. Unemployment and poverty are high; they are looking for aid from the UN under their Heavily Indebted Poor Countries act.

Zimbabwe, *1980*

This country separated off from South Africa in 1965. They had problems separating first from the UK, then from guerrilla warfare. The country settled down in 1980 and has had the same ruling dictator since. This dictator is known to be exceptionally brutal, often killing any opponents that try to run against him in an election, torturing children into following him and killing for him, starving the people, destroying the family/homes/business of anyone even thought to oppose him. The country was also involved in the war in the Congo, draining millions from that country. They are very poor and aid has been suspended because of the country's failure to meet basic goals and agreements. AIDS, infighting and a failing government is deteriorating the country.

Reference Page

The information in this book was researched and learned over an eight-year period. As a teacher, among many other things, I covered global events and presented information from around the world. This body of work emerged from these teachings. Hundreds of documentaries, websites, television programs, news programs and books went into the process, especially internationally, along with my own vast experience and knowledge. I could not name all of the resources used, but in my heart I am grateful to the many, many people in this world who fight hard daily to bring awareness and knowledge out into the world. This body of work is to help bring forth awareness, it is not intended as a statistical reference or a personal opinion.